Myth, Metaphor and Science

Myth, Metaphor and Science

Alan Wall

Including 'The Most Beautiful Experiment'
by Goronwy Tudor Jones and Alan Wall

Chester Academic Press

First published 2009
by Chester Academic Press
University of Chester
Parkgate Road
Chester CH1 4BJ
(http://www.chester.ac.uk/academicpress/)

Printed and bound in the UK by the
LIS Print Unit
University of Chester

A catalogue record for this book is available from the
British Library

ISBN 978-1-905929-73-3

Contents

Preface

The essays printed below are an attempt to approach certain recurrent problems in contemporary writing. What is the relationship between descriptive prose and scientific enquiry? How does the modern fiction writer decide upon the shape which a narrative should take? What is the relationship between form and language in poetry? Is metaphor in writing a choice or an inevitability? And is the first-person singularity of the writer an escapable condition, or one which it is intellectually irresponsible to try to evade?

These are large questions, and ones which I do not pretend to be able to answer. My own experience as a writer of fiction, verse and essays made me think that it was worthwhile to ask them, all the same.

I would like to thank the following for their assistance:

Steve Cook of the Royal Literary Fund for his patience and precision;

Anthony Rudolf for his generous responses to my unceasing queries, particularly in regard to poetry and translation;

Bernard Sharratt for continual entry to his encyclopaedic mind.

I am grateful to the RLF for appointing me RLF Project Fellow to enable me to produce these essays, and to the University of Chester for partial remission from teaching during the academic year 2007-2008. Some of the work here began when I was awarded an AHRB/Arts Council Fellowship to work with the particle physicist Goronwy Tudor Jones on the project *Extremities of Perception*. This work is ongoing. Gron has taught me all that I know about modern physics. Sadly, he has not been able to teach me all that he knows. Any mistakes are mine alone.

'Creative and Destructive Writing' was delivered as my inaugural address as Professor of Writing and Literature at the University of Chester.

Finally, I would like to thank Peter Williams of the Chester Academic Press for his generous assistance.

Putting the 'I' in the Middle:
A Few Thoughts on the Modern Essay

During the 1960s there occurred a phenomenon which became known as the New Journalism. Many names were associated with it, including Norman Mailer, Tom Wolfe, Joan Didion and Hunter S. Thompson. The writer foregrounded himself. He did not make any pretence to a dispassionate historical narrative, but instead said, 'Here I am, for better or for worse, right in the thick of things, with all my prejudices pretty much intact.' Dramatic presentation of one scene after another, with the writer's involvement clearly signalled, became the norm. Nothing has ever seemed quite the same since.

In *The Armies of the Night* and *Miami and the Siege of Chicago*, Norman Mailer strode through the events of his times, and described himself doing so in the third person. 'Mailer did this, Mailer thought that.' The device permitted not so much egomania as a curious objectivity. By not laying claim to objectivity, and by treating the self as one more subject to be examined and forensically described, a curious liberation appeared to be effected.

And yet how modern a device was this? This 'I' at the centre of things is, in one sense, the 'I' which has always occupied the centre of the essay. When Montaigne, who invented the modern essay as we know it, writes an essay, his qualification is effectively his utter lack of qualifications. He says that he starts from ignorance, and can do no other. Poking about inside the mental woodshed without preconceptions is what unspecialized essayists do. The more specialized and academic the essay becomes, the more it starts edging towards the monograph and the scholarly treatise. An essay in Montaigne's sense is by nature provisional. That is really what the word means. The French *essai* and *essayer* make the matter clearer.

Something is being tried. An attempt is being made. When we used to *assay* gold, we were using what was effectively the same word: we were testing the metal, to make sure it consisted of what it said it did. Proof quality precious metal showed that the metal had been tested and proven.

Montaigne makes a virtue of his lack of learning, his deficient expertise. He places at the centre of the world a particular 'I' whose very lack of specialized knowledge is his only qualification for writing, for testing the reality around him with intelligent scepticism, with a questioning which is untainted by either dogma or scholarship. In Auden's poem 'Montaigne', the poet writes, 'To doubt becomes a way of definition'. The poet's line is effectively pointing up the provisionality of the essay, the way it places reality in a parenthesis, a pair of brackets which will permit any manoeuvre of the mind within its mutual concavities. The essay lets the mind take itself for a walk, not knowing where exactly it will be going, or when precisely it is due back. The essay, unlike, say, the philosophical treatise, does not need to supply its foundational credentials before it gets started; it does not need to explain how it can know anything before it toys with the idea of asserting that it somehow does. It does not need to establish scholarly qualifications before arguing about scholarship, though it often helps if it gets the scholarship right. In Hazlitt's marvellous essays about Shakespeare, he frequently quotes the plays inaccurately. And yet, this is precisely where the strength of the essays comes from: Hazlitt was often quoting from memory. He was honeycombed with the works of Shakespeare. Had he not been so riddled in the language and characterisation of Shakespeare's works, he could not have written essays as inward with the texture of the plays. Academically this would be a problem: Hazlitt would be severely reprimanded these days for his misquotation. But his memorializing of Shakespeare (even including memorial contamination) is, essayistically speaking, magnificent.

It might help to think of the essay as a crux. This word, signifying any defining moment in a text or an argument, is also, of course, the Latin word for cross. So we have the sense of a vertical axis meeting a horizontal one. The vertical line is always that 'I' with which we started. The horizontal line might be any number of things - public affairs, a matter of principle, the history of science, a text in the canon, but the essay grows out of its encounter at a specific point with a personal obsession, personal experience, or an individual engagement with a text that might be available to all. Often the horizontal axis is something already in the public domain - a standard line of reasoning, or a particular body of work, so that the vertical axis becomes the individual negotiation of the matter presented to it. Anthony Rudolf's essay 'The Jew Etc.', published in the National Gallery's *Kitaj in the Aura of Cézanne*,[1] was the intellectual meeting point of a painter obsessed by writing and a writer obsessed by painting. If these were the vertical and horizontal axes of the essay, then the actual point of the crux was their joint obsession with the meaning of being Jewish in the contemporary world. Kitaj came to explore this topic ceaselessly in his painting, and Rudolf is still doing so in his writing.

We can look at another specific example, which is Gore Vidal's essay 'The Meaning of Timothy McVeigh'. This essay, collected in Vidal's book *The Last Empire*,[2] starts by recounting the public meaning of Timothy McVeigh, the man who was executed for blowing up the federal building

---

[1] Anthony Rudolf and Colin Wiggins, *Kitaj in the Aura of Cézanne and Other Masters* (London: National Gallery Company, 2001).
[2] Gore Vidal, *The Last Empire: Essays 1992-2001* (2001; London: Abacus, 2002).

in Oklahoma City, killing 168 men, women and children. He was a right-wing zealot, who had effectively declared war on the United States of America, and all the citizens who lived there. That is our horizontal axis, though for McVeigh himself it was the vertical 'I'. Now comes Vidal's vertical axis, the 'I' in the middle of the essay.

In the November 1998 issue of *Vanity Fair*, Vidal had written a piece about 'the shredding of our Bill of Rights'. McVeigh, in a Colorado prison at the time, read the piece, and then wrote Vidal a letter. The two corresponded, and it became evident to Vidal that the phenomenon of McVeigh was more complex and intriguing than he had imagined. The Oklahoma bombing took place on the anniversary of the killings at Waco, when a religious sect which called itself the Branch Davidians discovered that it had got on the wrong side of the lethal power of the American state. Here Vidal and McVeigh found themselves in agreement: the Waco siege showed federal agencies behaving in a manner beyond the law. McVeigh attended the Waco siege. He wanted to see what was going on. After he had witnessed the events there he was in no doubt that the US state was now out of control. And so Vidal's essay becomes an extended meditation on Timothy McVeigh and his dreadful protest against the antics of American domestic power. One form of murderous activity generates another. It is almost inconceivable that McVeigh acted alone in blowing up the federal building, but it suited the authorities to permit him to pretend that he had. His trial and execution allowed for that precious 'closure' so dear to politicians and state functionaries.

The Patriot Militias regard themselves as being at war with the US state. This was the world which McVeigh had entered, and it is a world sufficiently alien and threatening to most Americans to permit the immediate demonization of McVeigh. Vidal shows how his own attempts to think through the phenomenon of McVeigh and his actions were constantly thwarted by those who did not want any such 'thinking through' to occur. Given Vidal's own agenda in regard to the overweening American state, his interest in McVeigh looks suspiciously like solidarity. McVeigh even invites Vidal to his execution – surely one of the most prestigious invitations that can ever be extended, one moreover carrying no need to return the favour.

Vidal is a great essayist, but it could be objected that he is in a curiously privileged position, since he belonged to what is often called the 'Brahmin class' in America: those whose social position and contacts put them constantly in touch with figures elevated by power and prestige. Vidal can write about 'Camelot', the White House in the time of J. F. Kennedy, as an insider: he was there. He knew 'Jack' well. There are times when he seems to know everyone well. His vertical line can always call upon a wealth of personal experience and contacts. In his brilliant and hilarious essay on Howard Hughes, he starts by quoting his own father (a significant figure in the US aviation industry) as saying that Hughes was always a menace as a flyer.

So let us start from a humbler position. Here our vertical line is nothing but our own intelligence (Hazlitt, we should recall, did not begin from Vidal's eminent domain, though he managed to encounter some eminences as he went along). To write the essay that follows all you need is to read the newspaper, click on the Internet, and do some thinking:

Burning Books

It looks as though we might be in for another great epoch of book burning. The smell of scorched paper is beginning to drift over continents. Last year a group of neo-Nazis in St

Paul, Minnesota, gathered in the inner city to consign copies of the *Talmud* and the *Communist Manifesto* to the flames. A sideshow, certainly, but one can't help thinking that it might be as much rehearsal as nostalgic re-enactment.

For those who stoke the flames, it is invariably regarded as a form of intellectual responsibility. When Peter Abelard was obliged to burn his own books before being closely confined in a convent, it was to help him repent of his errors. Half a millennium ago, the followers of Savonarola burned every Florentine copy of Ovid they could lay their hands on, since those engaged in such fleshly metamorphoses were deemed to be breaching Christian protocol. Three decades later the Bishop of London, Cuthbert Tunstal, bought up, for burning (what else?), so many copies of Tyndale's English version of the Bible that he unwittingly financed many new editions. Robespierre wanted all the religious libraries to go up in flames, and found the time to make a serious start on the project himself. Fifty years ago in 1957 Wilhelm Reich died in prison in the USA. His employment of 'orgone accumulators' had rattled the administration, leading them to deposit six tons of the prophet's books and papers in a New York incinerator. And so it goes on. Outside sundry churches on the American continent, Harry Potter is being burnt even as we speak; guilty, apparently, of the promotion of necromancy.

Terence famously remarked that books have their fates (*habent sua fata libelli*), but the fate of certain books, their physical fate, still seems to be exemplary. In the special collection in Birmingham University Library there is a charred copy of the King James Bible. It still carries the faint whiff of a conflagration, even though the flames that ate into it were quenched over two hundred years ago. Inside its blue solander case it sits amidst the vellum bindings and the precious manuscripts, and when you take it out it almost falls apart in your hands. A not inconsiderable volume once, a large octavo, bound in rich calfskin with six raised spine bindings. But it has undoubtedly seen better days.

Not long ago I found myself holding this book and considering how it had once been in the hands of Joseph

Priestley; it might even have belonged to him – no way of knowing. In any case the flames that almost consumed it two centuries back were directed at him and his friends; directed at the contents of his mind, not the contents of the good book which stood proxy that night for his person. The date was 1791; two years since the French Revolution, which Priestley had supported. That made him, in certain eyes, pro-French, and being pro-French inevitably meant that you were anti-Anglo-Saxon. What goes around comes around. The aroma of Freedom Fries was already drifting over Europe.

This was also the great epoch of the isolation of the elements; the breaking down of matter into its atomic constituents. As John Dalton put it: 'I should apprehend there are a considerable number of what may properly be called *elementary* particles, which can never be *metamorphosed* one into another.' It seemed that you couldn't get any further down into matter than an atom. Now we know better. But Priestley had isolated oxygen, even if he did insist on still calling it dephlogisticated air. He was working out how things could burn in the first place – most things, even volumes of sacred writ.

So the burning of books does have a hallowed history. As a critique of the latest treatise, it is evidently an unsubtle technique, but its popularity nevertheless persists. Einstein's work was thrown into the bonfire volume by volume in the 1930s. Those eminent scientific sceptics, the Waffen SS, argued that since Einstein was Jewish, his theories regarding relativity and the photoelectric effect were racially contaminated and therefore untrue: QED. A similar logic must have applied to Freud: his writings were publicly burnt on the Opernplatz in Berlin in 1933. He had peered into the Aryan soul and found it wanting. The state of souls and the burning of books have been intimately linked through the ages: books had traditionally been burnt at the stake, along with whatever heretics had penned them.

Occasionally the burning was not *pro* superstition but *contra*: so in 1527, outside the Münster at Basel, Paracelsus added to the merry student auto-da-fé his copy of Avicenna's

7

medical textbook. He reckoned its effect on the minds of the young was deleterious, and he was right, as it happens. Regarding the advancement of medicine his gesture can be applauded, even if from a bibliographic perspective it left something to be desired. Twenty years ago, Salman Rushdie's book *The Satanic Verses* was burned in the streets of Bradford and Bolton by diligent Muslims who believed its words were evil. Book burners tend to be deeply untroubled by any qualms that they might be mistaken. Nor are they necessarily committed to close reading of anything other than their one chosen book. Unceasing repetition, of course, is not necessarily the same thing as close reading. There is even a specialized form of this activity: the burning of a manuscript before it can turn into a burnable book. At 50 Albemarle Street in 1824 the publisher John Murray burned Byron's *Memoirs*, without first reading them.

Heine warned us that wherever you start by burning books, you will end up burning people. His own books shared the fate of Freud's in Berlin in 1933. Ten years later his prediction had come true: people were being turned into smoke in his homeland, for what would now be called purposes of homeland security. Books have their fates, and they often augur the fates of the people who wrote them. We'd best keep a close eye on the flames. On bad days I sometimes think I can still catch a whiff on the wind of that charred Bible in the Special Collection at Birmingham.

No expert knowledge was needed to write this essay; all of the information contained in it is in the public domain. The vertical line of the essayist's activity consists of pulling it all together and shaping it into a coherent intellectual itinerary, though he did have his own experience with the burnt Bible in Birmingham. The essay is evidently not scholarly, and its chatty tone indicates that it is aimed at the press; but the placing of that vertical 'I' is crucial to it.

This pattern of personalization has, if anything, grown more pronounced. Books which would certainly not have 'turned personal' a few decades ago, do so now. Stephen Greenblatt's *Learning to Curse*[3] and Janna Levin's *How the Universe Got Its Spots*[4] both intertwine the personal with the impersonal matter under discussion, in one case Elizabethan literature and ideology, and in the other the formation of the universe. It is as though the vertical 'I' provides the spine which holds the body of discourse together in both books. After the initial shock of unexpected personalization, both texts soon start to feel entirely natural.

The genres of writing are shifting to accommodate the technique, but we should remember that the technique itself has been around for a long time. It was Montaigne's technique, which is where we came in, and it was also George Orwell's. The first sentence of the latter's essay 'England, Your England', written in 1941, was this: 'As I write, highly civilized human beings are flying overhead, trying to kill me.' That certainly introduces us to the vertical 'I'. It also introduces us to the hook.

'The hook' is actually a journalistic concept, but it is one which no writer, certainly no essay writer, can afford to forget. Let us make the distinction as clear as possible. Here is the beginning of a piece of writing about violence and statistics. First the opening with no hook: 'Statistics recently released by the government have shown that random acts of violence are increasing. Last year there was a 22% rise in what the report calls "unprovoked actions resulting in damage to property or human injury". That's

---

[3] Stephen Greenblatt, *Learning to Curse: Essays in Early Modern Culture* (1990; New York: Routledge, 2007).
[4] Janna Levin, *How The Universe Got Its Spots: Diary of a Finite Time in a Finite Space* (Princeton, NJ: Princeton University Press, 2002).

how you start without a hook. And here would be the start once the hook is put in:

> You are driving along the road, listening to the radio. Despite the cataclysms reported on the news, you have no particular reason to suspect that violence is heading your way. It is, though. In twenty seconds time a lump of concrete will be dropped from the bridge which you are approaching. The two 12-year-old boys who are balancing the ragged piece of masonry on the parapet do not know you, and have nothing against you. All the same, they will feel a sense of success if the concrete smashes your windscreen and sends your car careering out of control off the road.

After that we can start to talk about the statistics. A hook is another way of describing the necessity for a vivid opening to any piece of writing. If the piece of writing is an essay, then the hook can be either the horizontal axis - some matter of public concern - or the vertical 'I' that provides the personal dimension. Soon enough the two will have to meet. Then we will have the crossing point which all vivid essays explore.

Dilemmas of the Modern Fiction Writer

It seems to me that the greatest dilemma facing the contemporary fiction writer is the question of form. Our negotiation of form expresses our relationship with reality. If we continue to write a seamless narrative, untroubled by authorial scruple or perspectival query, then we are saying that the great tradition was never fractured, and that the discoveries and achievements of modernism in the arts were nothing but a side road, which can once more be safely ignored as we press on down the highway.

The Revolution

And yet there was a revolution back there, and I cannot myself see how any serious writer can afford to act as though it never occurred. Let us try to recapitulate briefly.

With a few notable exceptions, there have usually been three traditional ways to voice fiction: the first person, the third person, and the free indirect. I can speak as the person in the middle of the story, with all the implications of intimacy and limitation which that implies. 'Call me Ishmael,' Melville's protagonist tells us at the beginning of *Moby-Dick*, and we walk straight into his world. Mark Twain invented this tone of demotic urgency and partisan comradeship. The opposite voicing is that of the omniscient author, the third person with no limitation placed upon knowledge, since the God-like stance permits us to peer into all situations. Thus do we receive the legendary opening of *Pride and Prejudice*: 'It is a truth universally acknowledged, that a single man in possession of a good fortune, must be in want of a wife.' Who is speaking? Jane Austen, except that she does not have a name, and is not required to present us with any credentials. She knows everything; we agree to take that on trust.

The free indirect permits us to move between the omniscient narrator and the inner consciousness of the characters by shifting imperceptibly into the mind of one or other of the characters within the work. Jane Austen herself uses it. Most novelists use it to some degree. Without having to put the matter in inverted commas, we let the words on the page become those of the character herself rather than those of the omniscient author. Then along came James Joyce. Joyce radicalized the free indirect style to a remarkable degree. In *A Portrait of the Artist as a Young Man*, he disrupted all previous expectations about this voicing. Not only do we feel a moral and psychological shift, as we enter a character's consciousness; we now feel a fundamental linguistic shift too. The vocabulary and syntax, the whole linguistic world, move us with a jolt to an alternative centre of consciousness. Joyce first tried to write his *Bildungsroman* in standard form, surrounded by that all-encompassing narrative voice which we always hear in Jane Austen, and which critics sometimes refer to as the meta-narrative. That was *Stephen Hero*, a work which he abandoned. When he came back to the same subject to try again, he divided up his protagonist's development into five chapters, and the language of each of them shifts vertiginously. We sense from the articulation of the words that this is one mind and one life, but that it is changing at considerable speed, and as it changes the linguistic world it inhabits changes too.

The first glimpse we catch of Stephen is as an infant and he lives inside an infant's vocabulary and syntax: 'His father told him that story: his father looked at him through a glass: he had a hairy face.' Colon follows colon; parataxis follows parataxis. Short declarative statements succeed one another, without subordinate clauses, since young children think and speak declaratively. By the fifth stage of the book we hear the undergraduate Stephen uttering himself forth thus: 'The most satisfying relations of the sensible must therefore correspond to the necessary phases of artistic apprehension.' Never are we given a word of explanation as to how we move from one Stephen to another. The language itself provides the map. We must deduce from the language where we are situated in Stephen's life at any one time.

Fragmentation

And this radical style of situating us within the language of the narrator, rather than providing a meta-narrative which does the situating for us, is accompanied by the cinematic cut, which is an acknowledgment of the fragmentation of the overall narrative. The reason modernism was seen to be so potent was because such a deliberated fragmentation within the work corresponded to a fragmentation in reality itself. Modernity brought with it speed, unprecedented communication, urbanization and fragmentation. It is both chastening and exhilarating to consider that ours is the first civilization on earth to have a speed as its absolute. How can we join up the bits and pieces of such an accelerating world? Perhaps we can't. In which case the writing itself must not provide any phoney glue, in the form of a seamless narrative which ignores, rather than resolves, the fissiparous quality of modern experience.

Dickens in *Great Expectations* takes us back with unparalleled vividness to that moment in the graveyard when Pip is confronted by Magwitch. Yet, no matter how convincingly we are plunged into the horror of the experience, we are still surrounded by the possibility of a narrative voice which can situate and distance that experience, for the older Pip is ever-present, even if silently, with his calm and dispassionate vocabulary and voicing. We are never left entirely in Pip's mind, as this passage demonstrates:

> A fearful man, all in coarse grey, with a great iron on his leg. A man with no hat, and with broken shoes, and with an old rag tied round his head. A man who had been soaked in water, and smothered in mud, and lamed by stones, and cut by flints, and stung by nettles, and torn by briars; who limped and shivered, and glared and growled; and whose teeth chattered in his head as he seized me by the chin.

The structure of that last sentence is not a child's: the two semicolons alert us to a sophisticated syntax and grammar.

In Joyce's *A Portrait* the all-surrounding voice of the narrator is gone, which means that fragmentation and the cinematic cut are now inevitable. How else to take us from one stage to another? There is no voice outside the voices to provide an explanation. Fiction writers since have been forced to make a choice. Either revert to the Jane Austen position, or acknowledge in some way the modernist revolution. In what way must the form of fiction acknowledge the intellectual nature of the reality in which we find ourselves? Can it simply ignore it, and get on with telling a good story? Most popular writers have chosen the latter option. Reality never was fractured, or if it was, only a tiny group of intellectuals ever noticed the break anyway. So carry on as before. Yet some of the most intriguing and compelling modern writers do acknowledge the break, and find ways of writing through it, rather than simply taking a seamless detour.

Dilemmas of the Modern Fiction Writer

A Few Examples of Contemporary Fragmentation

Eliot registered the significance of Joyce's manoeuvre when he reviewed *Ulysses* and said that Joyce had found a way of imposing order on the great chaos of modern life and experience, by employing the Homeric parallel. The fragmentation of modern life and modern experience meant that if an overall resolving order was to be found at all, it would have to be imported from elsewhere; previous forms of art, for example, such as the Homeric epic. The interior monologue that Joyce introduced in this book found its formal control in a narrative pattern from two and a half millennia before.

Picasso seems to have arrived at a similar conclusion visually when he began to employ the expressive, non-realist, effect of primitive masks in painting *Les Demoiselles d'Avignon*. The abolition of chronology and the embrace of primitive form allow modern life to be fashioned into intelligible shapes, for how can we find anything but unrelated detail in a world of infinite fragmentation?

Michael Ondaatje is an example of a writer who, in his finest work, does not try to escape fragmentation but embraces it as one of his resources. In *Coming Through Slaughter* and *The Collected Works of Billy the Kid*,[1] there is no narrative, or at least certainly no single narrative. Different voices, different sources, give their evidence. Spaces are left between them. The white space on the page is one of the most important devices of the modern writer. The whole of *The Waste Land* is punctuated by gaps which are not to be filled by explanation or setting. The gaps announce a change of voice, and we must then deduce

---

[1] Michael Ondaatje, *Coming Through Slaughter* (1976; London: Bloomsbury, 2004); *The Collected Works of Billy the Kid* (1970; London: Bloomsbury, 2004).

15

from the internal evidence of the next speaker exactly where we are and who is involved. The technique is that of the mosaic. Fragments are brought together and begin to form a shape which is somehow bigger than all the fragments put together. Ondaatje is one of the most skilful deployers of the mosaic technique in modern fiction. He allows for a plurality of voices on the page, and does not put them into any hierarchy of significance by employing a meta-narrative. We as readers are left to glean who is speaking and where. We are situated amongst those 'plurabilities' Joyce spoke of in *Finnegans Wake*.

Janna Levin, in *A Madman Dreams of Turing Machines*[2] is not as radical in her technique as the Ondaatje of *Coming Through Slaughter*, but she lets us know that she is not Jane Austen. She recreates the lives of Alan Turing and Kurt Gödel, both brilliant scientists, both profoundly troubled, and both fixated on a poisoned apple. But she shows her hand, rather than trying to conceal it: 'Here I am, in New York City. It is the twenty-first century. This place is as good a place, this time as good a time, as any.' The author acknowledges her authorship, without in any way diminishing the vividness of the lives that are her subject.

Jill Dawson in her brilliant novel *Wild Boy*[3] acknowledges the clash of discursive voices and the clash of memories, without prioritizing one above another. We witness a collision of worlds. Victor, the wild boy of Aveyron, becomes a stage the adults march back and forth across. Can he be inserted into the world of language, having spent his early years outside language? In the years after the French Revolution this becomes a question not merely of one little boy and his needs, but of the validity of

---

[2] Janna Levin, *A Madman Dreams of Turing Machines* (London: Weidenfeld & Nicolson, 2007).
[3] Jill Dawson, *Wild Boy* (London: Sceptre, 2003).

the thought of the Enlightenment. Once again the gaps on the page, the white spaces, announce a new voicing. We are never informed that a new person will be speaking. We must deduce it ourselves. *Wild Boy* is a triumphant example of how a contemporary writer can acknowledge the achievements of modernism, and make use of them, without jettisoning all the benefits of a traditional historical narrative.

Elaine Feinstein adopts a different strategy. In her novel *The Russian Jerusalem*[4] the character starts in the present and is led into the past by the poet Marina Tsvetaeva. They travel back together to the time of the Stalinist purges, and meet Pasternak, Mandelstam and Isaac Babel. Tsvetaeva is Virgil to Feinstein's Dante, another superb example of how the modern writer turns to the past to find forms which make our present realities expressible. The journey to the Underworld becomes a way of approaching contemporary experience.

A different path altogether was pursued by those writers who have come to be known as magic realists. Theirs is a different technique: they let the light of the fantastic, the light of myth and legend, fall upon the seamless narrative and highlight the marvellous strands within it. By this means the homogeneous and rational world of the novel is disrupted and subverted from within. As their name implies, they are committed to a form of realism, but it is one which includes much of what this seemingly rational form would previously have excluded: the fantastic, the uncanny, the preternatural. The ghost story has collided with the realist narrative, and what spills out is a scene from Hieronymous Bosch.

Marquez acknowledges that this technique, this intellectual world even, began with Borges, whose stories

---

[4] Elaine Feinstein, *The Russian Jerusalem* (Manchester: Carcanet, 2008).

(for he never wrote a novel) problematize reality, and make us ask how we can ever accept any narrative as other than constructed. The deliberately traditional prose, often with footnotes and a bibliographic apparatus, or interrupted by deadpan scholarly digressions, is employed to undermine the reality for which it provides so many credentials and exemplars. This process began much earlier, with the great works of the eighteenth century, to which Borges was much devoted.[5] All reality has become a constructed narrative. We are now in a world in which Lawrence's famous injunction 'Never trust the teller; trust the tale' is cancelled out by Nietzsche's equally peremptory 'There are no philosophies; only philosophers'. Human identity often seems to be absorbed by the narrative it had assumed it was commanding. The tale swallows the teller, and goes in search of other tongues. We start to approach what philosophers call 'infinitized irony', where the ironic effect has no unironic certainty underpinning it. Each ironic distance simply seems to open up another, larger one.

In 'Tlön, Uqbar, Orbius Tertius', perhaps his greatest story, Borges imagines the creation of a land, a language, a history, a world. A phenomenally rich man effectively decides to reinvent reality, to reconstruct the world according to the dictates of a set of idealist principles. A single copy of the entry on the invented land, Uqbar, is then inserted into the *Encyclopedia Britannica*. Further data about the place and its philosophy will be forthcoming when a curious Englishman dies. Little by little we are given sufficient data to reconstruct the world they had constructed between them. The intellectual gymnastics are all put to a serious purpose. Borges would appear to have

---

[5] See the discussion of Pope and Swift in 'Creative and Destructive Writing' below.

written the story in 1940-1941, when a substantial part of Europe was engaged in rewriting reality so that it might fulfil the expectations of a particular ideology. Such fundamental disrespect towards reality is simultaneously beguiling and extremely dangerous. We begin to be horrified by it. The arcane story with its tangled bibliographical details becomes a political parable.[6]

Fictional form must be open enough to let contemporary reality in. If it closes itself entirely in a seamless narrative, with no possibility of fracture, then it refuses to acknowledge the great changes that have happened to our world, including the intellectual ones. In the inter-relationship between form and voicing, the writer places himself intellectually inside contemporary reality.

---

[6] One that is brilliantly analysed by Gabriel Josipovici in his essay 'The Plain Sense of Things', in *The Singer on the Shore* (Manchester: Carcanet, 2006).

A Note on Defamiliarization

The term was given to us by the Russian Formalists in the twentieth century. They were amongst the most intriguing thinkers on the subject of how literature actually works; how language become *literary*. Victor Shklovsky, who coined the phrase, was thinking of literature in mechanical terms; he wanted to know how a text works, in the same way that a mechanic wants to know how a car works – this is the analogy Shklovsky often used.

The Purpose of Defamiliarization

The aim is to set the mind in a state of radical unpreparedness; to cultivate the willing suspension of disbelief. We see and hear things as if for the first time. We see through the eyes, as Blake put it, instead of with them. In other words, the conventionality of our perceptions is put into question. We see the world afresh. This requires effort. We do not economize our creative effort in defamiliarization; instead we maximize it. By 'making strange' – *ostranenie* – we force the mind to rethink its situation in the world, and this requires an expenditure of effort.

The Formalists were fascinated by *Gulliver's Travels*; this was a founding text of defamiliarization. Swift lived in the century of lenses, and he decided to employ that fact imaginatively. Galileo had stared through his telescope back in 1610 and seen a universe vaster than any previously imagined, but he also saw the pockmarks on the moon's surface. The heavens were not a realm of perfection, as Aristotle had insisted. Later, Robert Hooke looked through his microscope and saw in vivid detail the features of the flea. An optical shift in both cases rearranged reality. Swift took the hint. Lilliput and

Brobdingnag are the imaginative rearrangements of reality; rearrangements we might see if we gazed upon humanity through either telescopes or microscopes. The perspective changes the nature of the humanity it situates.

All vivid writing is to some degree defamiliarizing. When Marianne Moore says of the swan that it 'turns and reconnoitres like a battleship', she defamiliarizes the movement of the swan through the water by an act of radical pattern recognition. All figures of speech aim to defamiliarize; to render the familiar unfamiliar. If they fail it is because they are either inept or clichéd. A cliché is a form of defamiliarization which has had its time and become familiar. Constantin Brancusi said that modernism in the arts had become a necessity because the techniques of realism were now 'a confusion of familiarities'. When our literary techniques become a confusion of familiarities, then we are seeing with the eyes instead of through them. It is time to employ defamiliarization once more.

Those writers who have been labelled magic realists are experts in the technique. Here is the first line of *One Hundred Years of Solitude* by Gabriel García Márquez: 'Many years later, as he faced the firing squad, Colonel Aureliano Buendía was to remember that distant afternoon when his father took him to discover ice.'[1] The present has become the future; the future the present. The first defamiliarization here is chronological. The second is in the form of a teleological thump: the man we are about to be presented with will one day face a firing squad. He will presumably be killed by execution. And finally, we are presented with the notion of having to discover ice, of being taken by your father to witness a natural phenomenon as though it were an exotic circus act.

---

[1] Gabriel García Márquez, *One Hundred Years of Solitude*, trans. by Gregory Rabassa (London: Penguin, 1970).

Myth, Metaphor and Science

When recording his album *In A Silent Way*, Miles Davis asked John McLaughlin to play the guitar 'as though you didn't know how to play the guitar'. The discarding of any superficial facility, so as to write as though we had not acquired a technique for writing, is the aim of defamiliarization. If it startles the reader it is probably because the writer has once more learned to be startled too.

Poetry and Form

Easter-Wings

Lord, who createdst man in wealth and store,

Though foolishly he lost the same,

Decaying more and more,

Till he became

Most poor:

With thee

O let me rise

As larks, harmoniously,

And sing this day thy victories:

Then shall the fall further the flight in me.

My tender age in sorrow did begin:

And still with sicknesses and shame

Thou didst so punish sin,

That I became

Most thin.

With thee

Let me combine,

And feel this day thy victory:

For, if I imp my wing on thine,

Affliction shall advance the flight in me.

This poem by George Herbert is an extreme example of lineation in verse. Prose does not specify its setting on the page. It is up to the typesetter to decide on the deployment and spacing of the actual words. As long as the words are printed in the right order, and with the right punctuation, the writer cannot complain. The situation is radically different with poetry and it is worth asking why.

Lineation in verse not only tells the voice how to speak the lines, but the reading eye how to read them too. Often enough, as in the case of 'Easter-Wings', it is more the latter than the former. Reading the poem out, without seeing the verse set on the page, would not convey the immediate sense we have of the shape of wings: one has to see the actual pattern to understand the full meaning of the poem. The poem forms a visual emblem of its own meaning; it demonstrates in a visual pattern what the words actually utter. Form and content are here clearly indivisible; the grouping of the words on the page is indispensable to the form of the poem. It is seeing on the page the lines 'Most poor/With thee' and 'Most thin/With thee' that emphasizes the sense of deprivation, of spiritual inanition, which is then revived into triumphant flight as the wings are outspread once more. This is a visual effect.

The words in verse cannot be separated from their lineation without a loss. We can see this easily enough if we re-lineate 'Easter-Wings':

Lord, who createdst man in wealth and store,

Though foolishly he lost the same, decaying more and more,

Till he became most poor:

With thee O let me rise as larks, harmoniously, and sing this day

Thy victories: Then shall the fall further the flight in me.

My tender age in sorrow did begin:

And still with sicknesses and shame thou didst so punish sin,

That I became most thin. With thee let me

Poetry and Form

Combine, and feel this day thy victory: for, if I imp my wing on thine,

Affliction shall advance the flight in me.

This is still verse, and there are still rhymes and an overall structure, but the intricacies of the emblematic effect are lost entirely. Had this been prose which had been reset in a different configuration from its original, we would almost certainly not have noticed.

Poetry at one level is self-consciously formalized language, language which has deliberately separated itself from daily usage in order to foreground its own resourcefulness. But here is where the difficulties start, since in another sense good poetry is always trying to escape that self-conscious formality which went before it, and which too easily identifies it as 'poetry'. The last thing good poetry wants to be is 'poetic', in the sense of an easily identifiable decorative use of language, one that has no function. In 1798 the language of *Lyrical Ballads* set itself in deliberate opposition to the allusive Latinate self-consciousness of much eighteenth-century poetry, which was more likely to say Phoebus than 'the sun'. The modernists at the beginning of the twentieth century were trying to escape the vagaries of a Symbolism which was all too likely to become vague and indefinable. Ezra Pound gives a specific example of what is to be avoided at all costs: lines like 'the misty lands of peace'. There is here, as Pound would have put it, no direct presentation of the thing, only soft focus gesturings towards grandiose abstractions. 'No ideas but in things,' said William Carlos Williams, or in other words: poetry should not be made up of abstract words softened by moody adjectives and adverbs. This temptation continues to this day, and bad poetry now as then is likely to be very similar to 'the misty lands of peace'.

And yet poetry is formally insistent, whether it is employing forms or using free verse. The very fact that the lines do not go to the end of the page, that the position of the words on the page is not simply left to a typesetter, indicates a care for the positioning of words in relation to one another, their rhythmic structuring, which leads us back, if we are prepared to go that far, to song; to rhythms so powerful that they were inseparable from music. It is such rhythmic potency, together with lexical astuteness and metaphoric inventiveness, which makes poetry so memorable. We are far more likely to carry lines of verse around in our heads than lines of prose. When we do memorize lines of prose it is likely to be prose that is closest in compression and rhythmic structuring to poetry – lines from the Bible perhaps, or a chunk from James Joyce's *Ulysses*.

So let us summarize the elements we are entitled to expect to find in poetry: compression, lexical fastidiousness, imagistic panache, and metaphoric inventiveness. Poetry chooses the right words, finds an order for them which is rhythmically compelling, presents us with original imagery, and makes connections which surprise us with their originality and justness. This last word is an important one. If poetry employs outrageous imagery simply for the sake of being 'original', we are likely to find it cloys quickly, however 'inventive' it might be. We want, to quote Ezra Pound, to find the surface detail in accord with its root in justice. We want poetry to tell the truth, however unexpected the truth might be. A respect for language informs the inventiveness of all good poets.

The Question of Rhetoric

How rhetorical is poetry? All convincing language is

26

rhetorical, and poetry cannot escape that condition. To what extent did Shakespeare's *Sonnets* dramatize and rhetoricize emotion exactly as his plays did? We do not know, and probably never will. 'I have been faithful to thee, Cynara! in my fashion.' Thus Ernest Dowson at the end of the nineteenth century, and we are surely entitled to translate the line as 'I have not been faithful to thee, Cynara! in any fashion whatsoever'. But given the clear hint of Roman decadence in the 1890s, the possibilities of off-the-shoulder togas at certain discreet addresses in Bloomsbury, we are also entitled to anticipate Cynara's reply: 'And I too have been faithful to thee, Ernest! in my fashion; i.e. not at all'. As Lear almost remarked: 'Here's two on's are sophisticated.' This is poetry as rhetoric and suasion; Yeats was greatly haunted by it, by the swooning cadences and the possibilities of verbal seduction. Later on, the 'modernist' Yeats sought to demolish both the rhythms and the rhetoric which he knew to be firmly rooted in his early verse, but he never quite escaped. This ongoing battle is, to one degree or another, the story of modern poetry. We have grown distrustful of verse which has explicit designs on us, whether erotic or political, and prefer a verse engaged in an exploration of itself and its world, negotiating reality in every possible sense, and ruthlessly examining its own use of language in the process.

But then, the anti-rhetorical stance can become a kind of rhetoric in its own right. Auden grew so accustomed to adumbrating the squalor of the human heart that the strategy starts to feel as predictable in its way as its grandiloquent opponent, and perhaps as falsely comforting. Late Larkin so frequently points towards the disaffection of love that one senses at times a certain love in the disaffection. Neither of these poets, however, breaches what is in effect one of the most important protocols of modern poetry, which is this: it must negotiate form without ever sacrificing authenticity of language. Should it depart from the natural word order of speech, then it must be with extreme deliberation, never merely to hold a rhythm or maintain a rhyme. Auden does so depart, and always with something like a hieratic effect: 'Let the more loving one be me'. He knows it is arch; the archness, in other words, is knowing and telling, not a lapse.

The Words

Good poetry repays any amount of attention; it never wears out. It is, in Pound's phrase, news that stays news. No examination is too minute for it. When Macbeth starts his speech 'To morrow and to morrow and to morrow', the repetition emphasizes the ceaseless locomotion towards a sequence of unchanging states. This is a mechanical progress towards succession, not success. Given what we know of Shakespeare's likely accent at the time, 'to morrow' would probably not have been much of a phonetic leap from 'to mort', and tomorrow itself, the sought-for and now dreaded future, has become indistinguishable from death.

Ernst Mach, the leader of that tendency in the physical sciences once known as Descriptionism, called science 'the economy of thought'. Poetry could equally be described as the economy of expression. Nothing extraneous or inessential should be contained in it if it is working to maximum efficiency. The potency of poetry comes not from any eschewal of metaphor, but rather from the acknowledgment that all language is inherently metaphoric. Even the plainest-seeming signifiers usually reveal metaphoric origins. The English language, declared the philosopher Ludwig Wittgenstein, is a graveyard of dead metaphors. Poetry at its best reveals an expanse of living ones, and even manages to resurrect a few defunct examples. In the chapter on 'Writing Science', we will see how Thomas Sprat in his *History of the Royal Society* sought to expunge 'this vicious abundance of phrase'; he here meant metaphor, the métier as he saw it of poetasters and prattlers, but he misunderstood what it is that language does.

Language does not merely grunt and gesture at the water. It is not simply a pointer; or if it is, it is also pointing to its own inherent creativity, its fecundity of imagery and cross-referencing. In Mach's 'economy of thought', water would be expressed as H_2O, which is to say a molecule in which two atoms of hydrogen combine with one of oxygen to produce that curiously forgiving and unbreakable medium known as water. Language immediately forms tributaries, not in contradiction to the constellation of matter known as H_2O, but in a paradigmatic expansion of association and possibility: riverbank, riverbed, riverside, riverboat. And of course we speak of time as a river, mimicking water's arrival and departure, its force, its constancy, its ability to deliver things to us and to take them away again; it has become a metaphor. And if we take the word river back to its Greek progenitor we will find the word for plunging down. How different all this feels from 'lake', something else made entirely out of H_2O, but plunging nowhere at all. How different again that word feels from loch or lagoon – all words to some degree cognate, but regionally differentiated, and therefore culturally distinct.

And here we come to an essential difference between that economy of thought which is science, and the economy of expression which is poetry: the former seeks to universalize itself into formulae, the latter to exploit the local richness of association which words afford. Another way of expressing this distinction is to think of the translatability of science compared to the highly problematic nature of poetry in translation.

Poetry operates at one level through metaphor, simile and the multiple associations which a word accrues about it. If we see the word 'pitfall', then in an industrial society there comes unbidden the horrific imagery of the mine (coal-mine, copper-mine, tin-mine) when a part of it collapses or someone falls down it. Broken bones, darkness, isolation. But in a society where no mineral mining had ever taken place, and where the pit was a hole in the ground, dug there so the lion might be beaten and netted into it, the word would be equally horrific, but for a different reason entirely: the victim would be trapped with an angry predator. Words gain their strength from their context. And there never has been a good poet who has not been an avid student of words. Poets are not exactly lexicographers, but they are always lexical obsessives.

A Note on Translation

Well, at least we know what it is we don't want.

What we don't want is a snail's pace transcription, deaf and blind to idiom and usage, of the sort that Housman parodied in his *Fragment of a Greek Tragedy*:

> *Chorus*: O suitably attired in leather boots
>
> Head of a traveller, wherefore seeking whom
>
> Whence by what way how purposed art thou come
>
> To this well-nightingaled vicinity?
>
> My object in inquiring is to know.
>
> But if you happen to be deaf and dumb
>
> And do not understand a word I say,
>
> Nod with your hand to signify as much.

Housman's target is a witless, if in one clinical sense 'accurate', movement from one language to another. This is the kind of literalism which, were it faced with French, would presumably feel obliged to translate 'Qu'est-ce que c'est?' by writing 'What is it that it is?' Language functions through idiom and metaphor. Frequently there is no exact translation possible for such an idiom or metaphor, though one can usually find a parallel of some sort.

Many modern writers have discovered a type of writing somewhere between imitation and translation. Thus we have Pound's Propertius, Lowell's Baudelaire and Arthur Waley's versions of the Chinese. We also have Christopher Logue's ongoing Homer. Such poems never transliterate; the poems must work as poems in the host language, which often means treating the visiting language cavalierly, or finding idiom to match idiom, rather than phrase to transcribe phrase.

Distinguished translators such as Christopher Middleton and Michael Hamburger, it should be said, have steered a course between the two extremes, remaining as faithful as possible to the original, while injecting all the native vigour which accuracy permitted into the translation.

When Pound, in the persona of Propertius, speaks of 'devirginated young ladies' who will come to enjoy his work, or points out that his cellar is not 'equipped with a frigidaire patent' the effect is, to use Pound's own recommendation, to 'make it new'. The last thing we want here is pastiche.

Metaphor

In science, metaphor is used to explain, test or visualize one (novel) reality in terms of another (less novel) one. A well-known example is the Bohr-Rutherford model of the atom in terms of the solar system: electrons orbit the nucleus as planets orbit the sun. The metaphor superimposes one reality upon another, and then asks a lot of questions to find out how well the superimposition actually works. If enough answers are negative, then a new model, a new metaphor, will be needed.

Metaphor in literature is very different. It describes one reality – a woman, say, or a landscape – in terms of something different. Underlying the difference must be a species of similarity, however exotic, or the metaphor does not work at all. The comparison must defamiliarize a known perception to some degree, or it will appear merely trite. The metaphor becomes exhausted in literature, unlike science, not when it yields too many inaccuracies, but when it has become so predictable that all the original defamiliarization has vanished. Then the metaphor has become a cliché and something new is needed to replace it. A cliché is a metaphor that has become undetectable; its distinctive perception has degenerated into triteness. For our purposes here, a simile is simply a loosely-bound metaphor, and no serious distinction will be made between them.

Inherent in both figures of speech, the metaphor and the simile, is a process of pattern recognition notable for its novelty. We notice a similitude, separated by difference, and we then fashion both elements into a single image in which our subject and its comparison are combined. A famous example might be Donne's pair of compasses.

If they be two, they are two so

    As stiff twin compasses are two;

Thy soul, the fix'd foot, makes no show

    To move, but doth, if th' other do.

And though it in the centre sit,

    Yet, when the other far doth roam,

It leans, and hearkens after it,

    And grows erect, as that comes home.

The pattern recognition here is radical. The comparison appears initially grotesque: the souls of two lovers are compared to a pair of compasses. But then Donne, with characteristic brio and panache, makes the image work. The compasses are endowed with some of the characteristics of the lovers. The phrase 'hearkens after it' is effectively using personification to imbue the compasses with feeling. This operates in the same way as the pathetic fallacy: with the latter, one attributes emotion and intention to nature, while here sentience and longing are attributed to a scientific artefact.

In Section Four of Mandelstam's late poem 'Verses on the Unknown Soldier', the poet talks of a ray of light with slanted feet balancing on his retina. The image is evidently that of a *saltimbanque*, a juggler and acrobat of the sort often painted by Picasso early in the twentieth century. They would balance on balls; Mandelstam has brought this image together with the idea of a beam of light made up of photons balancing on the ball of his eye. The image is as daring and provocative as Donne's. Its power arises out of its unexpectedness. Metaphor is crucial to poetry, as the linguist Roman Jakobson has argued in various essays,[1] but the metaphor needs to be highly inventive, and not merely mechanical.

We are looking here at pattern recognition used to fuse apparent dissimilarities into images of unity. The dissonance which is perceived, the apparent difference between the two elements brought together in the metaphor, is finally overcome by an ultimate sense of harmony and concordance, but the dissonance is essential to provide the image's energy. In other words, a metaphor, when inventive enough, creates a readerly *frisson* by employing as much dissonance as possible, while still redeeming the image into its ultimate coherence by pointing to a structural similarity that underlies the surface discord of the two components. When all that tension between the two parts of the metaphor or simile is lost, then the metaphor is dead: it has shrivelled into a cliché, because the dissonance has departed, and the remaining consonance has become no more than a frequently repeated comparison. There is no tension remaining to provide either the resistance or the recognition.

The momentary resistance, generated by our first encounter with a striking (i.e. successful) metaphor, is an acknowledgment that a new space, however tiny, must be created for it in the mind. A metaphor is a kind of oscillator, moving back and forth between two categories, two situations, two creatures, two planetary systems. Its pendulum effect generates a projective imagery which perceives or creates a similarity, or a shared identity, where none was previously noticed. The verbal oscillator institutes a dialogue between differences, which emerges

---

[1] See in particular Roman Jakobson, *Language in Literature*, ed. by Krystyna Pomorska and Stephen Rudy (Cambridge, MA: Belknap Press of Harvard University Press, 1987).

in a figure of speech, announcing some species of similarity, however remote that similarity might seem.

In my novel *The School of Night* I wrote this sentence: 'Fluked in a dawn light, London reinvents itself.' There are two metaphors working here. A fluke is a happy outcome achieved by chance. A snooker player aims for a red ball he wishes to pocket; he misses that ball, but the cue-ball comes off the cushion, finds another red, and pockets that instead. The player has been lucky. Happenstance has done his work for him. This is a fluke. In what sense, then, can London ever be fluked by light? If one is being 'strictly logical', then it cannot. Metaphor is here, as so often, ascribing intention where there is none. And then the second metaphor comes into play (to use a metaphor about the functioning of metaphor itself) and we have London reinventing itself. This personifies London, providing it with intention and intelligence. What is the purpose of the two images in this one line? The attempt to achieve vivid language. Metaphor defamiliarizes by generating energy in the language and a corresponding brightness in the imagery.

Such a seeming conflict between metaphor and 'strict logic' is what made Thomas Sprat in his *History of the Royal Society* denounce 'this vicious abundance of phrase'; by which, as we have noted, he meant figurative language, particularly metaphor. He was writing in the seventeenth century, not long after the Royal Society had been founded. The assumption behind his denunciation was that language could be voided of its figurativeness. It cannot. Language is inherently figurative and inherently metaphorical. There is a not a 'poet's language' which can be dispensed with, to be replaced instead by a 'scientist's language'. What the intelligent writer does is to exploit this inherent figurativeness of language, this metaphoric shape-changing energy inherent in language itself, and produce rich imagery out of it. Good metaphors, whatever else they are, are always expressive of intelligence and acute perception.

Attempts have been made to separate out the two elements making up a metaphor. I. A. Richards spoke of 'tenor' and 'vehicle'. It is hard to see how these distinctions help us much. More to the point, perhaps, is the fact that the more potent and unusual the metaphor, the more it will depend on delimiting the characteristics held in common between the two original elements. The word 'elements' here is metaphoric itself, so let us pursue the inherent metaphor. Two different atoms come together to form one metaphoric molecule. This can only happen, in language as in nature, if there is a shared logic between the atoms in the first place; some compatibility, however remote it might seem (think of Donne's lovers and the compasses). We are searching for a previously undiscovered isomorphic relation.

We saw how Marianne Moore spoke of a swan that 'turns and reconnoitres like a battleship'. Technically this is of course a simile, but for our purposes the metaphoric effect is worthy of remark. What are the two atoms that have come together here, to form our metaphoric molecule? The movement of a swan in water and the movement of a battleship through the ocean. These are the two atoms. Now the truth is that a swan is not really much like a battleship. It is much smaller, for a start; it is organic and covered in feathers; it does not contain sailors and there are no guns on its back. There is just one shared feature that the poet has settled on: a stately motion through the water, a long and graceful curve through the waves. And even here the imagery is operating at its limit, because battleships are not, in fact, much use for turning and reconnoitring: they are far too big. Much smaller boats are far nimbler for the purpose. If you are using a battleship to reconnoitre, then you have probably already lost your sea battle.

Rather than speak of 'tenor' and 'vehicle' with Richards, let us think of 'projective and interactive imagery'. Metaphor takes two separate images, projecting the implications of one image on to the other, and vice versa. In Marianne Moore's line, the swan has the image of the massive, stately battleship projected on to it. But she could, had she chosen, have continued back and forth with the projective imagery. She could have spoken of the sailors in the battleship's belly, or its webbed screws underwater, furiously thrashing while the ship retained its stately shape above the waves. Then the imagery would have been projecting from swan to battleship. She could have spoken of the swan's fuel driving it on; then the imagery is projecting from battleship to swan.

And here we come to an important point. The discussion has spoken so far as if we always have two intact and completed images, which simply allude to one another within the metaphor. Max Black, in his extensive work on the subject, was more inclined to think of metaphors actually creating the similarities which they display.[2] This is surely a useful way for the writer to think about metaphors. In other words, we do not simply reflect an existing similarity (however remote): we create one. The searching out of similarities here is dynamic and transactional.

To summarize the points made so far: a metaphor finds similarity in apparently dissimilar things or situations, and combines these different elements into a single functioning image, which retains both originals while transmuting them. It functions by projective and interactive imagery:

---

[2] See Max Black, *Models and Metaphors: Studies in Language and Philosophy* (Ithaca, NY: Cornell University Press, 1962).

aspects of one identity are imposed upon the other, and vice versa. This 'similarity' is often not so much observed as created, or at least partly created. This creation will often be taking place through the natural figurativeness of language itself.

The topographic metaphor

One of the commonest metaphors is the topographic one. We 'map out' thoughts or inter-relationships as though they were part of a place. These lines from 'Satyr' by John Wilmot, the Earl of Rochester, show the topographic metaphor in action:

> Reason, an Ignis fatuus, in the Mind,
>
> Which leaving light of Nature, sense behind;
>
> Pathless and dang'rous wandring ways it takes,
>
> Through errors Fenny Boggs, and Thorny Brakes;
>
> Whilst the misguided follower, climbs with pain,
>
> Mountains of Whimseys, heaped in his own Brain ...

Once the idea of reason as an ill-advised traveller moving across treacherous terrain begins, the imagery proliferates. Good writers, we should note, exploit to the full any metaphor's potential. So we have error, which reason is seeking to avoid, entrapping it in bogs and brakes, and then in that brilliant last line the topographic metaphor once more moves from the external landscape to the mental landscape (to continue the metaphor) inside the brain: 'Mountains of Whimseys, heaped in his own Brain...'

Cliché

If a cliché is a dead metaphor, then it does not always have to be buried. A metaphor can sometimes operate like one of those resurrection men in the nineteenth century, who were adept at removing corpses from their coffins.

Here is an example:

> I took a trip down memory lane.

This is obviously a cliché. Why? Because the phrase 'memory lane' has become over-used. We should perhaps remind ourselves that phrases become clichés, often enough, because they were such good metaphors in the first place; that's why they came to be employed so often. 'Memory lane' is a topographic metaphor, as is 'the flow of time'. But there might still be some life in it, if we accept the full consequences of its topographic origination. Let's make it a place again, as it was once when the metaphor was coined:

> I don't know about you, but I've taken to avoiding trips down Memory Lane. The place grows more shabby and urinous with every visit. Last time I went wandering down amongst the ruins, I was mugged. And do you know what the voice said, from inside its hood? "Given how little you've got, Missus, you're lucky I didn't kill you."

Metaphor and Language

Metaphors occur in language, but they are also frequently employing the figure of language as part of the mechanism. 'There's something about that landscape that really speaks to me.' 'Look at the way the two figures in the painting seem to rhyme with one another.' When Macbeth utters his famous words about the futility of life, the metaphoric tropes he employs relate to language:

> To morrow and to morrow, and to morrow
>
> Creeps in this petty pace from day to day,
>
> To the last syllable of recorded time ...

Time is uttering itself as a chronicle, a sequence of spoken moments, hence 'the last syllable of recorded time'. A few lines later Macbeth will speak of life as 'a tale told by an idiot, full of sound and fury, signifying nothing'. We can thrash about in language as much as we like, but if all our meanings have cut loose, as Macbeth's appear to have done, then our tale will be a parody of genuine signification.

One could go on listing types of metaphors, as Lakoff and Johnson do in *Metaphors We Live By*,[3] but the point should be clear by now. We noted how the philosopher Ludwig Wittgenstein said the English language was a graveyard of dead metaphors. His point was that dead metaphors are dangerous, because they shape our thought without alerting us to the manner and force of the shaping. He gives as an example Saint Augustine's troubled thoughts regarding the flowing of time. He points out that the problems Augustine appears to be addressing, about the nature of time, are actually generated by the figurative language itself. It is the metaphoric figure of time as a river which shapes any thoughts one might have about the 'actual subject'; in effect it *becomes* the actual subject.

---

[3] George Lakoff and Mark Johnson, *Metaphors We Live By* (Chicago: Chicago University Press, 1980).

An example might be the word 'gravity'. It was Isaac Newton who started using it to describe a universal law of attraction. If we say, 'Gravity pulls the object towards the earth', then we are actually employing a metaphor. Gravity has here been personified; it is an agency which is doing something, rather than the description of an observable phenomenon. We could easily be misled into talking about gravity pushing something in, which would be technically incorrect, since gravity, as an attractive force, must always be described as pulling.

Non-Visual Metaphors

We have spoken as though all metaphors are visual, and it is true that there is at least an element of the visual in most of them. But this is not always the case. If I say that someone is as good as gold, it is not really a visual metaphor, because gold carries its own connotations of value, whether or not we think of a yellow substance that has the number 79 in the Periodic Table. If I say her words were music to my ears, then this is not a visual metaphor at all, since it is impossible to visualize music entering an ear. Both these phrases are of course clichés, which is to say that over-use has drained them of any potency.

Conclusion

The good writer shapes metaphors which contain the maximum amount of dissonance or tension between two elements, while succeeding in finding a unity in the verbal image. In the process we see momentarily how language functions, how it shapes our perceptions, and how it offers that brief renewal of perception we often refer to as defamiliarization.

Creative and Destructive Writing

We have retained an unusually dated notion of creation. Often in the Psalms, God is compared to a potter, and sometimes to the potter who smashes his vessel into shards – the latter presumably because it exhibited imperfections. We will return to this. But even though the potter's craft requires that we hack something out of the earth, reshape it and then heat it to high temperatures, all of this is nothing compared to the process of creation which modern physics has been studying. At the very beginning of our universe, the temperature was too great even for the nuclei of helium and hydrogen to form, and certainly too great for electrons to be held by nuclei to allow atoms to form. Then the universe chilled sufficiently to permit helium and hydrogen nuclei to congregate their tiny parishes of energy into centres which could gather electrons around them. So now we have atoms. We have two elements. We ourselves begin to seem like possibilities, however distant, when at some point in the future stars begin to die. We are all of us the offspring of dead stars.

But in the earliest stages of creation, particles and antiparticles hurtle freely about, and collide with one another causing what scientists call annihilation. They can't actually vanish from the system and become nothing, as that word annihilation (with its *nihil* in the middle) implies; that is not permitted according to the law of the conservation of energy. But they cease to be what they were. Their energy re-emerges, reconfigured. Another way of putting this is to say that in the initial stages of creation, an immense amount of destruction takes place. If the potter's hand is shaping all this, then each shaping is matched by an equivalent smashing. Energy expresses itself as particles, which then annihilate one another in their collisions. At a temperature so phenomenal (a

43

hundred thousand million degrees) that the mind falters in trying to imagine it, there is no stable matter, only the transmutation of particles violently colliding; an energy of creation which is effectively indistinguishable from the rage of destruction.

It is worth remarking that the earliest cosmogonies seem to have been alert to this mating between creative and destructive forces. The Mesopotamian creation is followed by a deluge which obliterates most of what was created in the first place. And in an echo of that narrative, we have only reached Chapter Six of the Book of Genesis when the cataclysm arrives in the form of the Flood. The potter's eye, it seems, has seen its own creation and found it irremediably flawed. The pot will be smashed into fragments. The vivid imagination, what Coleridge called the 'esemplastic power', understood long before science could calculate and express the matter that creation and destruction are not separate realms: far from it; they constitute two hemispheres which only create a world when they are brought together. If creation and destruction are in fact opposites, then they are necessary opposites, dialectically dependent opposites. William Empson reminds us constantly throughout his work that the term 'opposite' is a troublesome late addition to human thought. The notion of opposition seems straightforward enough when used astronomically, to signify the position of two heavenly bodies with a difference in longitude of 180 degrees, but when used of creation and destruction, the matter soon clouds. 'A Truth in art is that whose contradictory is also true.' So wrote Oscar Wilde in his essay 'The Truth of Masks'. This was also the belief of the great Danish physicist Niels Bohr in regard to the important statements of science: if a truth is large enough, then its opposite is also true. When he was awarded the Danish Order of the Elephant, Bohr chose as his motto:

Contraria Sunt Complementa. Opposites complement one another. But to do so they need to retain all their critical force. Energy is only generated, as in an electrical circuit, when opposites are brought into communication. David Jones called his last great work *The Anathemata*, a word which is an emblem of its own meeting of opposites. The *anathemata* are the accursed things, which are also venerated, set aside, revered, made holy. As Regina Schwartz points out in her study of Milton, hallowing begins when something is set aside, and some etymologists have traced the idea of creation in Hebrew, *bara*, to the idea of cutting, dividing, separating.[1]

In art, said Picasso, one must always kill the father. We still remember *Les Demoiselles d'Avignon,* that quintessential act of the modern mind, as much for the vividness of its destruction as for the form of its creation. In any meaningful act of creation, we must continually be smashing things to bits. The potter hurls his vessel against the stone and it shatters into fragments. The god sees the flaw in his own creation and resolves to be done with it and start again. Wherever art can be said to have a history, then it is a history of the development of its own conventions to the point of destruction; otherwise there would merely be stasis, as there is for example in certain traditions, like that of icon painting. Such an art has a chronology which is additive and repetitive, rather than developmental. If the play *Hamlet* had simply obeyed the laws of revenge tragedy from which it started, then it would not be being performed, at numerous venues across the world, at this moment. The serious art we have grown used to views convention the way a butcher views a carcass. We have already quoted Pound's famous

---

[1] Regina M. Schwartz, *Remembering and Repeating: Biblical Creation in 'Paradise Lost'* (Cambridge: Cambridge University Press, 1988).

instruction, 'Make it new', and in his own personalizing way, Yeats agreed when he wrote: 'It is myself that I remake.'

So let me abandon all coyness forthwith and make the link. When what we call creative writing is bad, it is frequently so not because it is not 'creative' enough, but because it is not 'destructive' enough; not nearly destructive enough. It wishes to engage in a lengthy creative embrace with itself. It is flogging a dead horse and stroking a dead dog, when it should be digging holes for both rotting corpses and burying the pair of them. In the making of our universe creation and destruction are inseparable; in any form of serious writing, the same rule applies. Another way of saying this is to state that writing, whether it is deemed to be 'creative' or not, can never afford to be less than intelligent, and intelligence characterizes itself by constantly wielding the blade against its own certainties, flummery and effusions. It is not possible to be intelligent without being self-critical; it is sometimes possible to be inventive, exuberant, entertaining even, but not intelligent. Expression in writing must be complemented at all times by the critical instinct, which we might think of as intelligence in its destructive mode; the analytic mind does not trouble itself overmuch with pity, and all criticism – including self-criticism – is a form of analysis. When writing is entirely positive, without any destructive element, it will tend automatically towards sentimentality and insipidity; which is to say that it will be bad writing, though no doubt 'affirmative'. There is, of course, a kitsch of affirmation, just as there is a kitsch of sorrow and regret. Sentimental insipidity can characterize a piece of writing about child abuse (a recent favourite) as much as it can the intimate history of a favoured teddy bear. It is not subject matter, but style, which separates sentimental and bad writing from the asperities required of any intelligent composition in words.

There is a touching moment when Nathaniel Hawthorne and Herman Melville are walking on a beach near Liverpool. Melville, according to Hawthorne's account, had 'pretty much made up his mind to be annihilated …. He can neither believe, nor be comfortable in his unbelief; and he is too honest and courageous not to try to do one or the other.' Out of that struggle between the opposition of belief and unbelief came his finest work. Melville was dubious about those who want to say 'Yes' in literature, who wish to be purely affirmative; he championed instead those who say 'NO in Thunder'. In his book of poems about the American Civil War, he relates as much to the Confederate cause as to the Union, even though his political sympathies were very much in favour of the latter. The *anathemata*, we might recall, are things both beloved and accursed; both trampled down and elevated. Creativity meets the destructiveness of its own critique coming in the opposite direction: in Opposition, said Blake, lies true friendship. At the moment that Blake discovered this in writing, Joseph Priestley was discovering that such opposition facilitated the flow of an electric current, and a couple of decades later we would be treated to the neologisms *anode* and *cathode*.

Let us look at another, radically different, example of how destructiveness is part of the intricate threading of creation. Some of R. S. Thomas's poems are shorter, or certainly no longer, than many of the inscriptions chiselled on tombstones in a mason's yard. Why is it then that one does not usually expect to find any of the poet's lines included among the inscriptions on polished granite? One phrase should be enough to tell us: in his poem 'Carol' he speaks of 'charity's scarecrow', a phrase sufficient in itself to announce the destructive intelligence, that refusal to make all the required affirmative noises even at a time of

47

grief, that readiness to say 'NO in Thunder' which Melville so admired. Thomas's belief (and he was, after all, an Anglican clergyman) was troubled on all sides by doubt and self-questioning. This must have made him troublesome at times as a repairer of souls, but it is what turns his verse into poetry.

Walter Benjamin, in his essay 'On The Destructive Character',[2] spoke of the way in which destruction is necessary to clear a way through the debris which perennially surrounds us. This might be useful. We are all already situated in language before we ever start writing, not merely situated in it, but mired in it; saturated by a medium which is inescapable. Writing has to be critical, which is to say destructive, to clear a way for itself; otherwise it will remain merely a part of the mire. This is a unique difficulty of writing. Language for the serious writer has to become a form of resistance to the linguistic mire which surrounds us. It must challenge any conventionality of utterance. Such conventionality is the mire, and we should try to understand what that mire is: it is not the mire of witlessness; far from it. An astonishing amount of wit has gone into creating the mire, which aims to cajole and beckon and, in sinking us, to separate us from our critical faculties. Unintelligent in the larger sense it may be, but it is not short of cunning. A large part of learning to write is the process whereby we become increasingly critical of our own inherited usage, our casual daily utterance. The advice, 'You should write that down' never really works: writing has its own formal requirements, its own demands and necessities, and there are remarkably few people who speak with such precision that a literal transcription of their talk can be read

---

2 In Walter Benjamin, *One-Way Street and Other Writings*, trans. by Edmund Jephcott and Kingsley Shorter (1979; London: Verso, 1997).

satisfactorily at any length. The reason avid reading is inseparable from good writing is that one has to study how other writers have cleared a way through the debris, how they have fashioned a mode of writing, or a style if you prefer, through an intelligent critique of the language in which they find themselves located; through an unreadiness to let oneself off the hook, which is to say a painful avoidance of all the openings provided by linguistic predictability, and unconsidered utterance. This is a large part of the training of the writer.

Let us consider for a moment what Shakespeare does to King Lear, in a play which is surely a supreme example of 'creative art'. The old man goes from being a king of the land to being an exiled king of language. And he takes his chorus with him in the form of the Fool. Adding his own notes to the chorus is Edgar, *aka* Mad Tom, mimicking the ravings of a Bedlamite. What a high court of the realm they constitute between them now. What was meant to be an act of historic generosity, the king's headstrong insistence on dividing up his kingdom between his daughters, has instead turned into a catastrophe of insult and alienation. The one good daughter lives in exile while the other two, who have turned out to be no better than they should be, plot, manoeuvre and collude to humiliate the king, and to vie for the affections of Edmund. Just listen to the riot of creation meeting destruction head-on in this scene from Act Three, when this bare, forked creature is on the Heath with what is left of his retinue.

Edgar: Away! The foul fiend follows me! Through the sharp hawthorn blow the winds. Hum! Go to thy bed and warm thee.

Lear: Did'st thou give all to thy daughters?
And art thou come to this?

Edgar: Who gives anything to poor Tom? Whom the foul fiend hath led through fire and through flame, through ford and whirlpool, o'er bog and quagmire, that hath laid knives under his pillow, and halters in his pew, set ratsbane by his porridge, made him proud of heart, to ride on a bay trotting-horse over four-inched bridges, to course his own shadow for a traitor. Bless thy five wits! Tom's a-cold. O, do de, do de, do de. Bless thee from whirlwinds, star-blasting and taking! Do poor Tom some charity, whom the foul fiend vexes: there could I have him now – and there – and there again, and there.

Storm still

Lear: What! Has his daughters brought him to this pass?
Couldst thou save nothing? Wouldst thou give 'em all?

Fool: Nay, he reserved a blanket, else we had been all shamed.

Lear: Now, all the plagues that in the pendulous air
Hang fated o'er men's faults light on thy daughters!

Kent: He hath no daughters, sir!

Lear: Death, traitor! Nothing could have subdued nature
To such a lowness but his unkind daughters.
Is it the fashion that discarded fathers
Should have thus little mercy on their flesh?
Judicious punishment! 'Twas this flesh begot

Creative and Destructive Writing

Those pelican daughters.

Edgar: Pillicock sat on Pillicock-hill:

Alow, alow, loo, loo!

Fool: This cold night will turn us all to fools and madmen.

Two acts before, these had been kings, statesmen, favoured sons. All their needs had been legitimate. Now look at them. The glory of the language is brought about by the fracturing and laying waste of age-old social relationships and loyalties. Creativity and destructiveness are once more indissolubly joined.

It might be instructive for us to consider Alexander Pope's *The Dunciad*, one of the least sentimental, least spuriously affirmative poems ever written. John Ruskin thought it the greatest work of art in any form these islands had ever produced. Let us ask of that poem the questions we have broached above. Firstly, what is the debris Pope feels he must find his way through? What makes his creative writing so destructive that it has become exemplary? First off is the 'creative writing' that surrounds him. Here he is on the subject in his *Epistle to Arbuthnot*:

Fire in each eye, and Papers in each hand,

They rave, recite, and madden round the land.

No great enthusiasm for the churning out of verse as a therapeutic or life-affirming exercise here then. Pope examined it in terms of its competence, and found most of it severely wanting. 'Competence' in verse has grown harder and harder to judge, as expectations of strict formality have been abandoned, though I remember once watching the late Ken Smith making his way through a pile of entries to a poetry competition with a briskness which would surely have astounded the entrants. Twenty seconds per sheet was long enough to establish whether or not there was any serious engagement with the language here; whether the destructive element had met the creative one head-on, and parleyed. Most of the submitted 'poems' were merely mouthing the locutions of the time, this time in ink, and so could be summarily discarded. Samuel Beckett often made the distinction between writing and talk. So much of writing, in his view, was mere talk; talk that happened to have been written down; the age's prattle typeset.

In *The Dunciad* Pope borrows all he needs for structure and subject matter from Homer, *The Aeneid*, Dryden's *MacFlecknoe* and from the Lord Mayor's Procession each year in London. Then he gathers up every figure in literary life with whom he has had a quarrel (which was most of them, in Pope's case) and starts fashioning his magnificently poisonous phrases. It is the unforgivingness of intelligence, in its destructive mode of analysis and criticism, that fashions such a compelling imagery of denunciation. The constant associations of worthless productions in literature with feculent currents in the Thames, with dead or decomposing matter of one sort or another, produce a riot of invention:

> This labour past, by Bridewell all descend,
>
> (As morning-pray'r and flagellation end)
>
> To where Fleet-ditch with disemboguing streams
>
> Rolls the large tribute of dead dogs to Thames,
>
> The King of Dykes! Than whom, no sluice of mud
>
> With deeper sable blots the silver flood.

The creativity here, indeed what might also be called 'the beauty of the verse', is inseparable from its destructive intent and action. The 'silver flood' evidently conjures all the silver-tongued writers of antiquity, and the dead dogs who contribute their sable blots to the staining of that mighty tradition have become a metonymy for the pack of howling versifiers who rave, recite and madden round the land. To borrow William Empson's phrase about Thomas Love Peacock in *Seven Types of Ambiguity*, these are poets who first make a cradle and then rock themselves in it. Pope sees his job as going around making sure that, by the time he's finished, down will come cradle, baby and all. He can afford no sentimentality here, which is to say that every line of creativity must contain its quotient of animus; the creativity, which is considerable, is dialectically complicit with its own destructiveness. So it seems we are back where we started. This is how worlds begin.

Now Pope's target, Duncery, is hard to define, though we are undoubtedly confronted with at least as much duncery in our society as Pope was in his, and it requires all the destructiveness of a ruthless critique, all the forces of our analytic intelligence, to resist it. It might seem odd at first glance that the Roman Catholic Pope should choose a word so often hurled abusively at his co-religionists. The word derives from John Duns Scotus, the Subtle Doctor, who epitomized for the Reformers the hair-splitting refinements of the Schoolmen, those who had strayed altogether too far from what scripture and the primitive church offered and vouchsafed. As Tyndale puts it in his *Pentateuch*: 'They which in tymes paste were wont to loke on no more Scripture then they founde in their duns or soch like develysh doctrine.' Tyndale was not given to beating about the bush. And as late as 1581 in Marbeck's *Book of Notes*, the connection with Roman Catholicism is explicit: 'The Dunce-men and Sophisters...the inventers and finders, yea, and the very makers of Purgatorie.' By Milton's time the term is less denominational, though just as abusive: 'It were a great folly to seeke for counsel … from a Dunce Prelat' (*Church Government*).[3] But Pope's immediate precursor is undoubtedly the Dryden of *MacFlecknoe*:

> Even I, a dunce of more renown than they,
>
> Was sent before but to prepare his way.

The 'he' here is Shadwell, poor fellow. It really does not do to get on the wrong side of great poets in the history of literature: all anyone will ever recall of you is their superior rhyme and ridicule. For every person who reads a line of Shadwell today, a thousand others will recall Dryden's splendid rancour:

> The rest to some faint meaning make pretence,
>
> But Shadwell never deviates into sense.

For Pope the meaning of dunce and duncery has become ecumenical. It is now anyone whose incessant reasoning manages to obliterate rather than elucidate the object of study; or whose writing, however 'creative', is designed not to clarify existence, but merely to fill up the silence:

> Keen, hollow winds howl thro' the bleak recess,
>
> Emblem of Music caus'd by Emptiness.

There's still plenty of that music around, and it has not grown any quieter in the intervening years. The emblems these days blare out from the ringtones of mobile phones;

---

[3] All the quotations here are taken from the *Oxford English Dictionary*.

now there is a music caused by emptiness, if ever there was one, the emptiness of a volume of communication far in excess of any requisite content.

Lewis Theobald, Pope's first target, glosses and annotates Shakespeare to the point where Shakespeare disappears. There is undoubtedly a comfort to be had in antiquarianism, in the retrieval of those objects time has buried, in their collection and their annotation. One can easily spend a lifetime playing the antiquarian with Shakespeare, and rewardingly too; as long as one never forgets that the essence of Shakespeare is not antiquarian. He was the least antiquarian of writers, in that he grabbed what he wanted and needed from the past and made present use of it for his dramas. The famous clock in *Julius Caesar*, whether deliberated or not, announces that dramatic effect takes precedence over chronological exactitude. Pope would always emphasize the dramatic effect, where Theobald would merely footnote the anachronism.

And what of the *Variorum Dunciad*? It was Swift who first pointed out to Pope that most of his references would not be understood by any soul twenty miles outside the liberties of London. So why not attach notes of cod-learning, a scholarly machinery like that which surrounded editions of the classics, particularly Bentley's edition of Horace in 1710? Once Pope started on this gambit, he could not give it up, until with the addition of Book Four and the final *Variorum* of 1743, we have a book which is a mockery of books, a satire taunting all contemporary satires, a book which to a considerable extent presents itself as an anti-book. This is a book which foils its own forthcoming criticisms by preceding them. Pope gets his retaliation in first. Built into its text is a prolepsis of its own posterity. Now this had already happened, if in a different manner, with Swift's *Tale of A Tub*, another work which deliberately parodies the conventions of book creation, printing and footnoting, particularly in the fifth edition of 1710. In Pope's case, to begin with anyway, part of what is being mocked is that urge to annotate to death a living literature. Pope's first target, as we have seen, was Lewis Theobald, editor of Shakespeare, and in Pope's view a rabid over-annotator. That Pope is grossly unfair to Theobald is here beside the point; it is Pope we read two and a half centuries later, not Theobald. All serious literature is constantly meeting itself coming the other way, like the particle meeting the antiparticle in the moment of physical creation. All creditable 'style' is constantly putting itself into question. All intelligent books play with the idea of turning themselves into anti-books. Eliot asks himself in *Four Quartets* what the late November is doing with the disturbance of the Spring, and then he halts to remark that 'that was a way of putting it' and that it was 'not very satisfactory...' The function of this manoeuvre is to acknowledge that all writing is a manoeuvre; that there is no innocent place left to occupy in terms of writing as pure expression. We acknowledge, through self-consciousness, our indispensable knowledge of the tradition. And our self-consciousness should become a type of critique; which is to say, that our creativity is conjoined, inevitably, to destructiveness.

The identical strategy underlies most of *The Dunciad*, and the reversals between pious expectation and sordid reality are enacted through the dialectic of the couplet. Dialectics imply that reality is never single; that every statement effectively contains its opposite, that truth itself may be thought of as oppositional, complementary, an ongoing argument rather than a certainty placed beyond question. Questioning is at the root of dialectics, the Greek word for argument, and it is what makes the procedure radical, since that last word comes from the Latin *radix* meaning root. Insofar as writing is dialectical, it can never be creative without simultaneously being destructive; what it lifts up, it must also strike down. The venerated object must also be, in some sense, accursed, like Lear on the heath; or like the *anathemata*. The stateliness of the language in *The Dunciad*, the grand machinery of its rhyming pentameters, sets the linguistic stage as the mighty procession of the Queen of Dulness and her subjects sets the visual one, for a sequence of apocalyptic reversals. All our expectations about culture and enlightenment are turned upside down. The light at the centre of the word enlightenment is the lifelong enemy of the dullards and pedants and versifiers whose rituals and pageants Pope celebrates so darkly. The darkness is a brilliant one, and Pope even borrows Milton's phrase 'darkness visible' from *Paradise Lost*:

> Yet, yet a moment one dim Ray of Light
>
> Indulge, dread Chaos, and eternal Night!
>
> Of darkness visible so much be lent,
>
> As half to shew, half veil the deep Intent.
>
> Ye Pow'rs! whose Mysteries restor'd I sing,
>
> To whom Time bears me on his rapid wing,
>
> Suspend a while your Force inertly strong,
>
> Then take at once the Poet and the Song.

Before we leave Pope we might remark the precision of the verse, and his awareness that a good poet needs to be abreast of the thought of his time. That last couplet with its 'inertly strong' refers to the universal law of gravity, recently propounded by Isaac Newton, whose work the poet revered. Pope also made use of Newton's work on optics; as Maynard Mack put it, you will find in his work no confusion between the words effulgence and refulgence.[4] One of the most fatuous phrases ever uttered is 'poetic license'. A poet whose language is not in a constant search for precision is a bad poet.

Perhaps the most famous exemplar of the function of negativity in literature, certainly in our time, is Samuel Beckett. Beckett made failure and difficulty his theme. His recommendation regarding writing is terse and memorable: 'Ever tried, ever failed? No matter. Try again. Fail again. Fail better.' One might note that, although written in prose, this mantra is in fact a rhyming couplet. Beckett in *Krapp's Last Tape* hints at how he came to understand that the things he had been avoiding, failure and loss, were in fact his theme, once he'd had the courage to grasp them. The one victor in Beckett's world, whether dramatic or fictional, is always language. Language is inexhaustible. Its resources transcend any plot or anti-plot.

In one of the first stories he ever published, 'Dante and the Lobster' in *More Pricks Than Kicks*, the character Belacqua fails to translate Dante, fails to charm his Italian teacher into translating a troublesome passage, and fails to notice that the lobster he is delivering to his aunt, so that he might consume it with her later, is in fact alive. When he realizes this, he is filled with horror, to the dismay of his practical relative. She who cooks the lobster cannot afford to be sentimental; he who eats it can, providing enough distance exists between the two activities. Then he discovers how the creature must die: it will be immersed in boiling water, to extinction. Belacqua reaches for a little easy comfort, but the text itself contradicts him. Negativity overcomes the facile affirmation:

---

[4] Quoted in Marjorie Nicolson and G. S. Rousseau, *"This Long Disease, My Life": Alexander Pope and the Sciences* (Princeton, NJ: Princeton University Press, 1968), p. 266.

Well, thought Belacqua, it's a quick death, God help us all.

It is not.

Between the two paragraphs we see the dialectic in action. And we never do receive an adequate translation of Dante's phrase – *'qui vive la pièta quando e ben morte'* – which is perhaps untranslatable. We are back with the dialectic between the inscriptions in the mason's yard and the poetry of R. S. Thomas. Creativity in writing needs always to be wary of itself; destructiveness is its necessary complement. *Contraria Sunt Complementa.* In the opposition between the creative and the destructive force in writing lies our only hope. Take away one and you have sentimentality, mawkishness and kitsch; take away the other and you have cynicism, which rapidly becomes as wearisome as kitsch. Creativity separated from destructiveness leads to that fatuous affirmation of which Melville was so distrustful; destructiveness without creativity is the voice of resentment. Resentment is a fascinating subject, indeed a motor of history, according to Nietzsche, but it requires a whole book to itself.

Myth and the Modern Writer

Why are modern writers so obsessed by myth? Why do they return to mythic themes, rewrite them, effectively create new versions of our oldest stories?

Why was Ted Hughes at the end of his life writing his own, free version of Ovid's *Metamorphoses*? Why before that had he produced a version of Euripides's *Alcestis* and Seneca's *Oedipus*? In one sense, the answer to the question in relation to Hughes is more straightforward than it might be with other writers. He was fascinated by classical tragedies because he'd found himself living inside one. Not one but two female partners were to commit suicide, the second including their daughter in the act of immolation. In *Alcestis* the queen offers to die in place of the king, Admetos. One can see how the subject might not so much have fascinated as tormented him. But Yeats produced versions of the Oedipus plays too. Derek Mahon has written his own *Bacchae*, Seamus Heaney has written versions of Greek plays, Robin Robertson recently produced a version of *Medea*. Pasolini made extraordinarily compelling film versions of both *Oedipus* and *Medea*. Our contemporary culture is obsessed with repossessing and reworking the mythic material of the past. We are permitted to ask why.

Seamus Heaney recently produced a version of *Beowulf* which has become a best-seller across the world, and in 1971 John Gardner published a remarkable novel, *Grendel*,[1] which was a rewriting of *Beowulf* from the point of view of the man-eating monster. It is perhaps the Gardner version which might lead us most usefully to the theme of the contemporary writer and myth. What Gardner did was to use the original legend as a heuristic principle, a route of

---

[1] John Gardner, *Grendel* (1971; New York: Vintage, 1989).

discovery, a way of probing our assumptions about ourselves. We take the myths, the earliest and often most potent stories we have ever told about ourselves, and we defamiliarize them. Defamiliarization is frequently an optical device – think of *Gulliver's Travels* and those tiny and huge people in Lilliput and Brobdingnag. By seeing something from a radically different angle, we see aspects to it which convention had made previously invisible. The coarseness of humanity's habits when seen through an optic the size of Tom Thumb's is the defamiliarizing device of Brobdingnag. Now, this is what Gardner does in *Grendel*: he uses the monster's viewpoint to critique the heroics of humanity. Their boasts and boozing in the mead hall are seen from the stance of an outsider. He is in a unique position to gainsay all their accounts of him, and their myth-making in regard to their various encounters. He lives in a world of appetite and terror, but he also lives in a world of language. He is a linguistic creature and therefore able to tell his own story. And his own narrative seems inexplicably contemporary; he becomes the existentialist of Anglo-Saxon dread. Though he is outside and alone, yet he is mysteriously a member of the linguistic community. This mixture of ancient source and contemporary language and sensibility is at the heart of our modern reworkings. We intermingle the present with the past; this mixture, this incongruity, a species of intellectual miscegenation, generates energy.

At the beginning of Hughes's *Alcestis*, Apollo describes himself as 'the maker of the atom'. Atomism was already a philosophical possibility at the time Euripides was writing; Leucippus and Democritus were atomists. But the playwright did not write this line. What Hughes is doing here is to try to make the language of the play as vividly contemporary as possible. Part of the defamiliarization functions as a linguistic shock: we retain plot and character, but fill the new version with contemporary insight; Grendel as an Old English existentialist filled with dread, and expert in contemporary usage, or Apollo as the maker of the atom, with all that that means for a post-Hiroshima reader.

We should remark here that we have altered our view of myth. *Mythos* itself simply means story, so we began to identify the earliest stories ever created and called that study mythology. James Frazer's *The Golden Bough* coincided with the high point of imperialist expansion and possession. Myths in his account are clearly the versions of reality held by those not in possession of scientific knowledge. Wittgenstein complained about this reading of myth as if it were merely a fumbling and mistaken version of science: 'This is too big to be a mistake,' he remarked, and we are more likely to sympathize with Wittgenstein nowadays than with Frazer. One of the reasons for this is that we live after that movement in the arts known as modernism. Just as Frazer was completing his mighty work, Picasso was discovering that the forms of modernity might need to borrow the forms of the primitive for their own purposes. And this is what we have been doing ever since, in art, music, dance and literature. Instead of patronizing myth and the primitive, we realized how much we could learn from them.

We saw how Constantin Brancusi complained that realist art had become 'a confusion of familiarities'. The primitive, the mythic, permitted the shattering of all that convention. Suddenly we saw distinct form in all its uncompromising luminosity, and all else became inessential. Mythic shapes and patterns cast such mighty shadows on the cave wall of the imagination that they could be used to obliterate many of the unwanted niceties of scrupulous realism. *Les Demoiselles d'Avignon* is still the astonishing painting it was a century ago because of its brutal energy, its unattenuated shapes, its lack of interest in anything but the presentation of vital form. A modern man paints a 'primitive' picture, and when, much later, Picasso was to be taken down to see the Palaeolithic cave paintings, his comment afterwards is revelatory: 'We have invented nothing.' It is interesting that of two of the most famous plays from the 1950s, *Look Back in Anger* and *Waiting for Godot*, it is surely the latter that has transcended its initial context. The Osborne play now looks knotted in the very skein of convention it was thought to be escaping, whereas Beckett's play has the spareness and vitality of myth. One could say 'modern myth', but that merely begs the question, since myth, if compellingly retold, always feels either modern or timeless.

We have dusted the myths down: better stories have never been told. More realistic ones might have been fashioned, and more sophisticated ones staged, but no one has ever created stronger narratives or stronger characters than those the myths present to us. So, since it is a cliché that no new tales can ever really be told, why not return to the old ones, and see what a contemporary sensibility, psychology and language might make of them? In describing what he saw as the psychic conflicts in the minds of the Viennese he was treating, Freud reached back to Oedipus. He saw in the myth a universal applicability which had never been superseded by subsequent science. When T. S. Eliot wrote *The Waste Land*, he too reached back to the same mythic material. A typist is seduced sordidly in a bedsit in London. And Tiresias describes the scene, he who has seen it all before so many times, he who, having been both a man and a woman, can see things from both sides – not that such duality seems to improve anything. In both cases, Freud and Eliot found a form through which contemporary existence could express itself, and the form was borrowed from myth. Both Oedipus and Tiresias appear in Sophocles.

A myth can be used in the manner of Walter Benjamin's 'dialectical image', which contains the present and the past simultaneously. In this it should be distinguished from that type of historical fiction which might be more aptly described as historicist fiction; which is to say that it operates on the premise that it is possible to reinhabit the past authentically, without acknowledging the existence of the present in the writing – as though the modern writer can simply disappear, an agency that has become invisible. Louis MacNeice believed this to be impossible. As he writes in *Autumn Journal*: 'It was all so unimaginably different/ And all so long ago.' The use of myth permits the acknowledgment that it was unimaginably different, and thereby acknowledges the unimaginableness of the present too. Both our origins and our existence here at the end of time are equally monstrous, equally unimaginable. This is why Borges wrote in his short parable about Don Quixote and Cervantes, 'Myth was there at the beginning of literature, and it is at the end of literature too.' In myths we discover both the monstrous and the marvellous.

The modern writer made the decision to enter myth, rather than merely see it as the shape of earlier people's belief. Myth simplified that 'confusion of familiarities' which Brancusi detected in modern realist art. It allowed for an expressive and monolithic formality. Think for example of Stravinsky's *Rite of Spring*, with its young girl dancing herself to death to ensure fertility's continuance. Eliot uses Tiresias as the focusing consciousness of *The Waste Land*, and Pound begins his *Cantos* with a section from Homer.

Inventiveness can then be inventiveness about character and language and perception; the shape of the narrative is given. What Joyce borrows in *Ulysses* is the shape of the classic tale, and the order of characterization. His form is now provided. All his modern inventiveness proceeds to fill the pre-existing structure, which is large enough to accept the mass of contemporary data. Eliot saw this work as the end of the novel as we have known it, and one can see why. It was the beginning of 'the mythic method' in fiction.

If the myth is to live, then it must represent an opportunity for a journey, possibly even that most exciting of journeys, the one to the museum. Two of the most fascinating artists of our time, the film director Jean-Luc Godard and the painter R. B. Kitaj, have both testified as to how their imaginations first came alive inside the museum. All the writer's current resources must be brought into play; there should be no hint of pastiche. In his book *The Sacred and the Profane*,[2] Mircea Eliade talks about the *axis mundi*, the sacred pole which shaman communities placed at the centre of their villages, the centre of their world. It connected the highest and the lowest, connected up the realm of heaven with that of the underworld, humankind's habitation being situated midway between them. This axis located the community in cosmic space, situated it in what was otherwise a homeless homogeneity. Eliade discusses many different manifestations of this pole, employed to centre existence in the vastness of unwelcoming space. In one village, the pole goes right through the centre of the ceremonial house, exiting through the roof. The shamanistic figure, dedicated to the furthest explorations possible in the most far-flung realms, would climb the pole during the ceremonies of initiation. This spiritual journeyer is thus gifted with the ability to connect up heaven and hell; he can now make the ultimate journeys that the rest of

---

[2] Mircea Eliade, *The Sacred and the Profane: The Nature of Religion*, trans. by Willard R. Trask (1959; Sydney: Harcourt, 1968).

the community is unprepared for, but need to have made for them nevertheless, for purposes of both solace and ultimate information.

It is an instructive and intriguing image, and a psychic pattern that recurs in many different forms in different times and cultures. In a sense, what the shaman does in climbing the pole, in the trance-like state of his initiation, is parallel to what Dante the poet does through his dream vision in the *Divine Comedy*: he visits heaven and hell and the regions between. He makes the ultimate journey and returns with the necessary images and information for the rest of the community to locate itself, and thereby orientate itself within the totality of existence. Poetry has often performed this function. In Book VI of the *Aeneid* we have a descent to the underworld, and much Romantic and post-Romantic poetry involves a visit to one sort of hell or another, counterpointed by the occasional glimpse of paradise. Coleridge's 'caverns measureless to man' recur with continued hallucinatory force in Baudelaire and Rimbaud. The earliest epic we have, *Gilgamesh*, contains a journey to the underworld. Human curiosity, it seems, must touch the extremities of perception, even if they lie beyond death.

Such an *axis mundi* locates the centre of existence as its ordering truth. But what is the *axis mundi* of our modern scientific world? We might usefully ask if it was replaced by Galileo's plank, down which he rolled his metal balls and so measured their velocities. In fact, Galileo used all sorts of surfaces and implements to arrive at his various conclusions, but for the sake of imagistic economy here, let's stick with his plank for the moment. Is this then our modern myth, or does it seek to replace all myth? This plank is resolutely unenchanted. It facilitates observation and close measurement. It lets you conclude that $F=ma$, which is to say that a force can be calculated by multiplying the mass of the body with its acceleration, or the other way about. Watch closely and you will discover that gravity is evidently a uniform force when applied in the same place, since objects fall at the same rate, whatever their size. Galileo's plank, placed at the centre of our scientific culture, seeks to become the new *axis mundi*, and so the centre of the world, which is to say that all our perceptions about the world are about to become scientific. So does this then constitute a replacement of myth, or does the myth simply evacuate itself to other, more welcoming, sites? What we are asking in effect is, what's the story, since we have already remarked how the Greek word *mythos* originally meant story. The world is about to grow larger and more marvellous, whichever *axis mundi* you employ, since Galileo is about to look through his telescope and see an unimagined vastness. At that moment the *axis mundi* is his 'optic tube', the same one that will soon enlarge Milton's imagination.

And yet what Milton writes in *Paradise Lost* is surely more mythic than scientific, despite the reference to Galileo and his telescope in Book One. For a long time Milton thought that his epic would take an Arthurian shape, but he then became dubious about the authenticity of the Arthurian legends. Another way of expressing this would be to say that his imagination could not actually live inside them. It is not, after all, as though he could go to the muniments room and pull out authenticated documentation about Satan's Fall from Heaven, but he could believe these mythic narratives, all the same, more than he could the others. The Fall legends provided him with structures his imagination could move around in, and which could provoke and facilitate the full force of his language, in a way he had come to feel the other mythic narratives could not.

Myth, Metaphor and Science

Myth is liberating. It offers shapes and characters and structures which do not need to dispense with the science which is such an indispensable aspect of our modern consciousness. As Apollo shows, when he appears in Hughes's *Alcestis*, the myth can incorporate the science that has come after it, not to dilute but to strengthen itself. The dragon in Gardner's *Grendel* performs the same function; it exists in all times, and therefore has access to all knowledge. It knows all about contemporary physics. What one can never afford is an awkward fumbling at a culturally distant authenticity, the sort of uncomfortable language that comes across merely as gaucheness. A. E. Housman parodies this mode brilliantly in his *Fragment of a Greek Tragedy*, already quoted earlier in 'Note on Translation'. It has to be said that Seamus Heaney's *Beowulf*, despite its breathtaking popularity, does not entirely escape Housman's stricture. In its determination to stay faithful to reference points and metre, the verse often creaks in a manner that Heaney's own poetry would never permit. People speak to each other on the page in a way they would surely never have done on the street or even in the mead hall.

Rilke, when he first encountered *Gilgamesh*, felt that he had found something entirely new and wonderfully fresh; it was the same response that Picasso had had to the Palaeolithic cave paintings. Something had been achieved long before with an authority which both artist and poet were searching for in their own modern locations. Rilke said *Gilgamesh* was the first epic of the fear of death. Reading a number of versions of it I became fascinated too, and decided to try my hand. This has now been published, together with a book called *Jacob*,[3] which combines an account of the patriarch of that name in the Book of

---

[3] In Alan Wall, *Gilgamesh* (Exeter: Shearsman Books, 2008).

Myth and the Modern Writer

Genesis. It seems to me that all I have said above became relevant in the writing of this long poem: it had to feel contemporary as well as ancient, its language needed to be idiomatic and compelling, and it had to be able to incorporate later knowledge and discoveries without losing the narrative thread or excitement of the original. The original poem was set in what we would now call Iraq, where a war was taking place. So I had sections like this:

In the *battue*, beaters press lions on

Until they are netted. Tricky should one of your netsmen

Prove unsure of his knots.

Or if you set out by underestimating the lion.

The gods sit in council. [*]

In an oval office they sit

With a Bible open at a page in Exodus

Describing salvation for a few;

Slaughter for many.

Huwawa dead.

The Bull, the hit-man, slaughtered.

How will this go down in heaven,

Amongst the statistics of apocalypse?

How should Halliburton calculate the outcome?

Will zeroes in ledger books burst their skins?

Surely Enkidu must die.

Gilgamesh is royal. He can live -

Say, Hirohito in 1945 on the Chrysanthemum Throne

Myth, Metaphor and Science

While MacArthur makes all the running
Out there on Tokyo streets.
Like the Japanese, Babylonians obey orders:
Thus the wisdom from above, then as now.

They mutter darkly in conclave.
Papers are signed.
International calls are made, discreetly.
Men in suits speak softly in corners.

Suddenly Enkidu falls sick
Like Arafat, poisoned perhaps in his compound
Or Litvinenko lit up inside
By radiation's
Malevolent candle.
That wound from Huwawa
Had the essence of darkness inside it.

Enkidu:

It will be lonely in the grave
Between the Tigris and the Euphrates
Without you there smiling or shouting.
Saddam will be there, of course,
Entangled now with the spirits of his victims
Like a cat coming up from the cellar
Its face bejewelled
With gossamer from cobwebs.
Still, no point killing him twice.

Myth and the Modern Writer

And Gilgamesh:

I'd rather die than walk about up here without you.

Enkidu asked if no wisdom
Could be gleaned from the gods.
Gilgamesh turned his face towards the sky and squinnied.

'They're planning a catastrophe,' he said finally.

'Are we in it?'

'Everyone's in it. All whose names appear in the Book.'

Then Enkidu began to curse:

Let the hunter's fingers be broken in his traps.
Let the harlot Shamhat
Have her womb sealed
So that no life can go in
And none come out.

And Shamhat answered softly:

I gave myself to you. You were glad to have me then.
Why do you curse me now?
Why do men always curse
What they want so badly

When they cover you with kisses?

Then Enkidu:

Forgive me, Shamhat.

Let men die inside you each day

So others might live

The others they kill as soon as they leave your temple.

What strikes me now looking at that section of the poem is how my preoccupation with Gilgamesh enabled me to think about the present-day goings-on in Iraq. It was not as though the present was being pasted on to the past; not at all. The use of the myth is liberating precisely because it provides us with a literary structure large enough to contain the present, large enough to let us see the present vividly, in a defamiliarizing light.

There is one final option open to the modern writer: to challenge the myth, to confront it with its untruthfulness in terms of what we now know. This is the strategy of *The Penelopiad*, where Margaret Atwood takes *The Odyssey* and allows women their voice. Penelope and the hanged handmaidens return at the end of history to have their say, a say the original text never permitted them. They have been wronged by the narrative of history and tradition, and must now supply voicings for the myth which have previously been missing. This is effectively also Anne Stevenson's strategy in her version of *Medea*.[4] Here the accusation is explicit: Euripides was lying through his teeth. Here Medea is allowed to confront Euripides himself

---

[4] In Anne Stevenson, *Stone Milk* (Tarset: Bloodaxe Books, 2007).

with the version of herself he perpetrated and tradition has accepted. As she says to the Chorus:

> Don't you see that every ugly thing you've heard about me –
>
> My every wicked deed, so called, and treachery –
>
> All, all are inventions of ambitious men?

The Corinthians, it seems, paid to have lies written about her; myths as always have territorial ambitions, and provide territorial excuses. And so in the short verse play, subtitled 'An Entertainment', the *Medea* of Euripides is replaced by the *Medea* of Medea. She was always voiced by men and now returns at last to voice herself, while the men must listen. And finally there is an admission of the inventiveness of myth, its fictiveness, the way it forms intellectual shapes to make sense of things, and such senses can change in time. At one point in the drama Medea exclaims that no woman would put her boys to death the way Euripides portrays it, but one might surely question this. Magda Goebbels did precisely that: she poisoned her little ones rather than hand them over to a world without Hitler. Curiously enough, this happened in the same year that 'the sun incinerates a city' (the end of Corinth in this alternative version of the myth): that event is the one we refer to as Hiroshima. Once again, the myths offer unlimited inventiveness.

It is one of the great tragedies of twentieth-century literature that T. S. Eliot did not continue with the extravagant linguistic inventiveness of *Sweeney Agonistes*, that slice of jazz age drama, simultaneously mythic and modern. Instead the language modulated into the stage acceptability of *The Family Reunion* which, despite a certain potency, has lost the feistiness of the earlier fragments.

Myth, Metaphor and Science

What one is hoping for in mythic writing is to convey the myth, to translate the legend, but without ever taming it.

Writing Science: Part One

The problem from one side can be stated thus: is language so inherently metaphorical, so incorrigibly figurative, that it cannot be ultimately aligned to a scientific description of reality? And has modern science, in particular quantum physics, become so mathematical in its conception and expression that any linguistic statement of quantum realities can never hope to be more than a loose approximation to the truths discovered in the last century? We have seen how, when Thomas Sprat wrote his *History of the Royal Society,* he believed metaphor could be expunged from writing altogether. He believed metaphor to be an unnecessary surface decoration, an embellishment with no function but the distraction of insufficiently focused minds. Since then we have come to see language differently, and now realise that metaphor is inherent in language. We cannot avoid it; we can only stay alert to the potency of its manoeuvres, and attempt to use it to our profit, rather than being imprisoned within it.

Just how quickly the metaphoric agency can become invisible is evident in a notion like natural selection. Darwin himself was aware of the danger inherent in this term, in that it seems to imply an agency, an intelligence even, where what is being described is in fact a vast accumulation of natural processes, whose result can be described metaphorically as though it were a selecting agent, like a pigeon fancier who prefers a certain size and shape of bird, a particular length of beak, etc.; this is one of the analogies Darwin actually uses, in order to explain the matter to himself. Add together all these processes throughout evolution and you end up with the survival of those mutations of species best suited to thrive in their specific environments. How easily though, in saying 'natural selection', we think instead of an intelligent agency inseparable from Nature itself, making choices, and dispensing with those who have not met the requisite standards. What is 'Nature' here anyway, but a personification, an anthropomorphism, in other words a different type of metaphor? It is effectively the same personification as that used by Alexander Pope:

> Nature, and Nature's laws, lay hid in Night;
>
> God said, Let Newton be! and all was light.

Nature here seems to be perilously close to Andromeda, the female prisoner about to be rescued by the Perseus of science. Richard Dawkins, the devil's chaplain to the devil's chaplain, constantly speaks of the 'pitilessness' of nature. The term is meaningless, though, except by metaphoric extension. We can only speak of pitilessness where pity is possible. I can say that Creon behaved in a pitiless manner by refusing to let Antigone bury her brother, but I can hardly say that the lion behaves in a pitiless manner in eating the gazelle. The lion is merely being itself. This is what lions do; there is no ethical choice to be made, because human ethics are inapplicable to lions. It is inherent in the leonine state that a gazelle is a moving object to be halted, torn apart and consumed. Similarly, Dawkins in ascribing pitilessness to that set of laws and probabilities we call for convenience Nature is blind to his own inherent metaphor. Blindness here is a metaphor too; there's no escape from them.

Blindness to metaphor: this is everywhere the problem. The biggest metaphors we live inside tend to become invisible, and we take them for reality. Perhaps this is what Plato was getting at with his allegory of the cave-dwellers taking the shadows on the wall for reality. We mentioned how Wittgenstein, in a brilliant piece of analysis in *The*

Brown Book, shows how Augustine's difficulties about the meaning of time in *The Confessions* all stem from his sense of time as a river. Because this metaphor is built so deeply into Augustine's psyche, he does not believe it is a metaphor at all; merely an accurate description of reality, an expression of knowledge. So he thinks of time as flowing; he thinks of the present as existing at one point on the map, with the past upstream of it, and the future downstream. Out of this topographic notion of time as geographic location with a current flowing through its terrain arise all his conundrums. In other words, the linguistic expression and its concomitant metaphor create a set of consequences, imagistic and logical, which are implicit in the usage. We must analyse the usage to discover those implications which otherwise seem merely 'natural'. Unless we can come to understand the metaphors we are inhabiting, we are entrapped by them. This is the burden of Wittgenstein's later philosophy.

So, given this inherently metaphoric nature of language, can it ever convey scientific truth? Many scientists have said, 'No'; only mathematics can properly convey reality with the requisite precision. But the great Danish physicist Niels Bohr said over and over again: 'We are suspended in language.' He was addressing his fellow scientists, alerting them to the danger that science needed to translate itself out of equations and into a language comprehensible to non-specialists, if science were not to become hermetically sealed inside its own preoccupations. Insofar as it is possible, the achievements and considerations of science should be expressed in a language intelligible to all. It was Bohr who invented the term 'complementarity' to describe the nature of modern physics – its discovery of wave-particle duality, for example – and the complementary half of Bohr's statement could be this: 'We are all of us sustained by science.' If the scientists are suspended in language, the non-scientists are implicated in a world of scientific discovery and development. To be entirely ignorant of this world, our world, is to be ... well, ignorant. Writers cannot afford such ignorance. An ignorant writer is, *de facto*, a bad one. Swift could never have written *Gulliver's Travels* without his fascination with the *Transactions of the Royal Society*; Pope understood the distinction between effulgence and refulgence because of his interest in Newton. He could not get very far with the *Principia* though – very few people in the world could. And just to make the point even more sharply, Newton never permitted an English version of the book to be published in his lifetime. The first one came out three years after his death. He had, he said, not wanted to be troubled by 'smatterers'.

From the *Principia* on, the situation gets worse. Modern science is formidable. The endless supply of volumes popularizing science shows the great hunger for some understanding of the achievements and discoveries of modern physics and cosmology. To write such science books one has to be a scientist. The problem is one of expertise. Much modern science does not yield up its secrets easily. To understand modern physics and cosmology with real depth you would need to be a sophisticated mathematician. But our age has seen the greatest proliferation of 'understanding science' books ever published. Why? Because the achievements of modern science (not just technology, but science as knowledge) are utterly astonishing. To be uninterested in them would be to be uninterested in life. This, after all, is where we can understand what we are made of, what forces shaped us, and how the words 'matter' and 'energy' are different ways of expressing the same matrix of existence.

Although there are earlier candidates for the title, Roger Bacon in the thirteenth century for example, most of our historic accounts date the birth of modern science to the time of Galileo. This was the moment when we shifted from the geocentric and Ptolemaic view of the world to a Copernican and heliocentric view of things. One can see how this took a lot of swallowing. We feel stationary enough, standing here on the earth. We do not appear to be hurtling about the heavens. And the Christian scriptures were read as confirming the fact. When Galileo was summoned to Rome in 1616, Cardinal Bellarmine drew his attention to what we would now call Psalm 19, where the sun is described as moving about the sky in its excitement before the Lord. So tradition and common sense informed the world that heliocentrism must be wrong. This was not the first time such ascription of error from *magisterium* to working science was to happen, nor was it to be the last. Galileo was looking through his telescope and arranging his planks so that balls could run down them (they went at the same speed, whatever their size, so Aristotle had been wrong about that). In other words, Galileo was treating all of the material world as subject to examination, scrutiny, measurement and investigation. There was no map marked, 'This is sacred: no enquiries here', as early maps had designated the unknown, and perhaps unknowable, parts of the world with the legend, 'Here be monsters'. When Galileo looked through his telescope and saw craters and protuberances on the face of the moon, he knew that the system known as Aristotelianism was now dead for ever, since it had declared the heavens to be a sphere of perfection and immutability. Those pockmarks on the lunar surface signified changes and collisions with other celestial bodies. They meant that the same laws applied up there as apply down here, something that would be demonstrated with seemingly incontrovertible force when Isaac Newton published *Principia Mathematica* in 1687. Interestingly, for the writer, Bellarmine sought to contradict Galileo's discoveries by pointing him towards another (substantial) piece of writing: the one we call the Bible.

This history of modern science makes for very exciting narratives. When a novelist as gifted as John Banville wrote two novels, *Doctor Copernicus* and *Kepler*,[1] he showed how well such material lends itself to contemporary writing. But you have to buckle down and do some serious reading. The mention of Newton reminds us of what we said earlier: modern science can be formidably difficult. Not many people could read *Principia* in his lifetime, and not many can read it now. And things begin to get even worse in the nineteenth century. Once James Clerk Maxwell starts formulating how electricity and magnetism form one united field of force, electromagnetism, science becomes increasingly dependent upon mathematical expression. The facts about heat, for example, those thermal realities which were so important for calculating the efficiency of steam engines, and the waste of energy that was too often involved, were presented as statistical realities rather than dynamic ones. This is to say that the reality of an observed phenomenon can only be measured and properly expressed by looking at it in terms of a large amount of data rather than observing a single trajectory, or one particular aspect of the phenomenon. This privileging of the statistical over the dynamic, of the mass of observable data over the itinerary of the one individual datum, becomes even more fundamental in quantum mechanics.

The development of science often dictates the metaphors which predominate at a given cultural moment. If we traced the history of a number of words in English, we would see how the intellectual paradigms in which we

---

[1] John Banville, *Doctor Copernicus: A Novel* (London: Secker & Warburg, 1976); John Banville, *Kepler: A Novel* (London: Secker & Warburg, 1981).

are situated at any one time change the very nature of our lexicon. For example:

Atmosphere

Gravity

Atom

Electron

Each of these words changes its potency and significance according to the state of scientific knowledge and agreement. The notion of atmosphere meaning a pressure of 14.7 lb on the square inch, available according to the *OED* from 1830, would not have been possible to earlier ages without the means of measuring it. Gravity simply meant weight or heaviness, a meaning retained in our Latinate *gravitas*, until Newton's great discoveries. He decided to name the universal attractive force *gravity*, and that meaning has remained with us ever since.

The notion of an *atom* (from the Greek word for indivisible) as the ultimate component of matter goes back to Greek antiquity, to Democritus and Leucippus, and only came to be fully accepted in the West in the seventeenth century. To call yourself an atomist in England in the 1590s could still have proved dangerous: it was to declare yourself part of the avant-garde in thought, possibly one of those who professed Copernicanism too. Those at the centre of power were not keen on such decenterings. Towards the end of the nineteenth century the word undergoes a transformation. It is discovered that the atom has a structure, that it is not indivisible. The meaning now starts to contradict its own etymology; this is common enough with words, and such a contradiction complicates the original metaphor beyond recognition. In the 1890s we discover that the atom can be divided further: there are electrons inside it. And why did we elect to call those elementary particles that? The Greek word *elektron* meant amber, which when rubbed will attract little bits of paper and wool to itself, thus exhibiting the force we call static electricity. William Gilbert wrote a treatise on the magnet in 1600 and began to use the word *electricam*, which finally ends up as our electricity. The negatively charged elementary particles which orbit the nucleus inside the atom are named after the amber which was first observed having 'electrical properties' two millennia before.

Looking at the four words we have given as examples, we can see the ceaseless interchange between scientific definition and metaphor, and how such interchange can confuse the relation between a scientific description of reality and a metaphoric use of language in non-scientific writing. If we read in a novel the line, 'The atmosphere between them had changed', we can be pretty certain that, whatever else is meant, the writer does not mean, 'The pressure on them both was no longer exactly 14.7 lb per square inch'. Similarly with gravity: a writer is far more likely to be using the older sense of *gravitas* in employing the English word in normal usage: 'He informed me, with some gravity, that there was something I should know.' A knowledgeable enough writer might write the following line: 'The force she exerted on his mind at this time was as unrelenting as the force of gravity on his body, and as unforgiving.' *Atom* is also likely to be used in the old sense of units of indivisibility: 'If we break this down into its individual atoms...' As for *electron*, it is unlikely to be used except for deliberate effect in non-scientific writing: 'Flies orbited about the rotting meat like electrons around a nucleus.' Far more likely is the use of the word electricity, and once again the usage will probably be metaphoric in a non-specific manner: 'The old electricity between them had died.' If we insist upon precise scientific definition here, the usage will become ridiculous: 'Harry was the anode, and Sue the cathode in this relationship...' Some metaphors have to be given a permitted space in which to function, and will simply resist too great an exactitude of interpretation.

Some years ago I was confronted with this problem in dramatic form. I was awarded an AHRB/Arts Council Fellowship to work with the particle physicist Goronwy Tudor Jones. We had elected to write a book together. The book was to be entitled *Extremities of Perception*, and started from images taken from the Hubble Telescope and bubble chambers in CERN. In other words, the largest things and the furthest things in the universe were to be contrasted with the very smallest things, elementary particles, and the way we imaged both realities was to be compared and contrasted. I began this project with an insouciance made possible only by complete ignorance. Little by little, it started to dawn on me what a mighty task we had taken on, though I suspect that Gron had always wondered about the viability of the book. It has never been published.[2] Sixty thousand words rest quietly in my files, awaiting a more accomplished revisiting, possibly in a different lifetime. What I finally offered as completion of the project was instead a novel, *Sylvie's Riddle*, and two books of poetry, *Alexander Pope at Twickenham* and *Gilgamesh*. This was a more than adequate completion of the Fellowship, but it might be worth looking in detail at one of the problems we encountered.

Gron and I wrote a joint presentation called 'The Most Beautiful Experiment' (which appears below), in which we spoke about the double-slit experiment with electrons, often thought of as the most elegant experimental

---

[2] Though see Alan Wall and Goronwy Tudor Jones, 'Extremities of Perception', *Leonardo, 39* (2006), 467-8.

demonstration ever conducted. What it demonstrates is wave-particle complementarity; in other words, how electrons can behave as both waves and particles. This duality, or complementarity, is the mystery enshrined at the heart of modern physics. All of the scientific knowledge here came from Gron, not from me. My job was to try to use whatever skills I had as a writer to convey as compellingly as possible some of the knowledge contained in my scientific collaborator's distinguished brain. Now, at a certain point, we wished to convey some sense of how atoms can only exist in certain quantum states. Using the hydrogen atom as an example, since it is the simplest of the atoms, with only one proton and one electron, I wrote the following sentence: 'Were it not for the quantum states, the negatively charged electron would collapse into the nucleus, and the atom would be abolished.' Gron could not accept this sentence, partly because he was not happy with the word 'collapse'. It carried an implication of a gravitational force, whereas the forces concerned were electrical. So here is the description we finally agreed upon:

If electrons were really orbiting the nucleus as planets orbit the sun, then they would be losing energy constantly in the process – this is what Maxwell's electromagnetism tells us. But if they were constantly losing energy then the electrons would spiral into the nucleus and the atom wouldn't form. So how is it then that the electrons don't make it down as far as the nucleus? The answer to that question lies in wave-particle complementarity and the quantum states.

It is less immediately striking than the original sentence, but it is truer. And note that the atom here is not 'abolished'; instead, it 'wouldn't form'. This attempt at scrupulous exactitude has made the project simultaneously fascinating and difficult. Aligning one's usages of language with scientific acceptability is a painstaking and lengthy business, and probably represents one of the greatest challenges facing any writer who tries to write about science.

A thought struck us as we worked. The original double-slit experiment was conducted with light by Thomas Young in 1803 at the Royal Institute. In one sense it was an exercise in pattern recognition. Earlier, in the chapter on metaphor, we looked at how pattern recognition lies at the heart of metaphoric perception: we see similarity in dissimilarity and form a striking image out of it. This is precisely what Young did when he noticed that the interference he was observing when two sources of light met each other was parallel to the interference patterns one can see in water when two sources meet. And exactly the same ability for radical pattern recognition was to be employed by Young a decade later when he started decoding the Rosetta Stone. Patterns that could be detected in the Greek, which could be decoded, must be reproduced in the hieroglyphics, which at that point could not be understood. The same abilities were being employed in realizing that light propagated itself as a wave and identifying the significance of a cartouche on a hieroglyphic inscription.

Niels Bohr became famous for never making any statement without immediately qualifying it. It is hard to make unambiguous statements in language. Think of one of our normal statements: 'If things had turned out differently....' Things didn't, of course, it being in the nature of things not to. The little idiomatic phrase contains a metaphysical conundrum. We know that things always turn out the way they turn out, and that the notion that they 'might have turned out differently' is always by way of a lament that things, as ever, turned out precisely the way they did. There is, of course, a way of using the phrase to think about events: it is called alternative history. You start from a premise: for example, what if Hitler had won the war? But to do this in science requires us to rethink nature and reality in a way that seems almost whimsical. Such rethinking often takes the form of science fiction or SF. And the best SF tends to be written by people with some scientific knowledge. Their rethinks are invariably literate and informed.

The problem might be seen at its simplest by looking at the phrase, 'a quantum leap'. We say, 'The politician made a quantum leap there', meaning he made one of the biggest jumps he possibly could. Quantum leaps first came into atomic physics to describe how light is emitted when an electron 'makes a transition' (jumps) from a high energy level to a lower one within an atom – emitting a quantum of light. On the scale of phenomena known in the universe, this is tiny. One can see why some scientists are driven back to expressing their truths entirely in mathematics.

The Explanatory Analogy

There is probably one law we can state about scientific writing whose purpose is explanatory. Images from the known realm will be used in an attempt to elucidate the more difficult realm requiring exposition. This can be done by analogy, simile or metaphor. So in trying to explain the inner workings of the atom, to themselves as well as to others, Rutherford and Bohr modelled its workings, by analogy, on the planets orbiting the sun. The analogy broke down quite quickly, because the electron on this planetary model should be constantly shedding energy. But see how we take imagery from what we know well and apply it to what we are exploring. One old and famous example was the comparison of atoms with billiard balls in motion. Atoms are hard to break, like billiard balls, and so the well-known characteristics of the known object were employed to describe the nature of the more elusive one.

The best writing in science finds the most vivid analogies, the most striking similes, the most arresting metaphors. It is, in other words, engaged like poetry in pattern recognition. The biggest difference is that metaphor in science seeks to familiarize, whereas in literature it tends to defamiliarize.

Writing Science: Part Two

What follows is an essay on complementarity written by the particle physicist Goronwy Tudor Jones of the School of Physics and Astronomy at the University of Birmingham and Alan Wall. It is offered as an example of writing which makes every attempt to be scientifically literate while remaining at all times available to the non-scientific reader.

A version of this paper was given jointly by the authors at the Description and Creativity Conference held at King's College, Cambridge, in 2005.

Writing Science: Part Two

The Most Beautiful Experiment

Goronwy Tudor Jones and Alan Wall

1

The Two-Slit Experiment with Electrons

Ask nature one kind of question, you get one kind of answer. Ask it a different type of question, you get a different type of answer.

Here we have the essence of what is sometimes called wave/particle duality, which is in fact an aspect of complementarity. And the experiment which exemplifies this doubleness at the heart of nature is the double-slit experiment with electrons, originally a thought-experiment dreamt up by the great physicist Richard Feynman, which was later performed. Its original purpose was to provide a conceptual non-mathematical introduction to quantum mechanics. Its ultimate performance gave exactly the results Feynman had predicted, and it was recently voted the most beautiful experiment in history. So what is it?

We fire electrons at a screen which has two slits in it. We know that the electrons are tiny subatomic particles, so they should form little piles in front of the wall behind the screen with the slits in, just as they would if they were bullets. That's what they'd do if they were behaving as we expect particles to behave (*Fig. 1*).

But what we actually get is something quite different, something so extraordinary that we must rearrange our notion of reality to acknowledge it. What we see shows us that the electrons are not obeying Newton's laws of motion, as bullets and cricket balls do (*Fig. 2*).

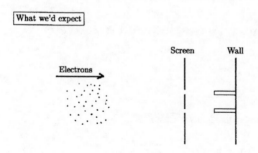

Fig. 1: Result expected if electrons behaved like Newtonian particles

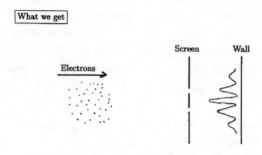

Fig. 2: Result obtained is totally different from Newtonian expectation

What we are seeing here is that the subatomic world is curiously different from our everyday, macroscopic Newtonian world, and the clue to understanding it is to study the undulating pattern of arrival points of the electrons at the wall. What we are seeing is something we know from elsewhere, namely the interference patterns observed in water if we drop two pebbles on to the surface at the same time.

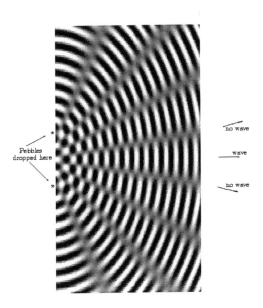

Fig. 3: Wave pattern caused by 'interference' of the waves from the two pebbles

In *Fig. 3* we see the recurrent patterns: first a strong wave going to the right, then a weak one on either side at about 15 degrees, then another strong one... If two equal waves meet, crest with crest and trough with trough ('in phase' to use the physicist's jargon), they double their size; but if, where they meet, the crest of one wave arrives with the trough of the other, and vice versa ('out of phase'), then they cancel each other out. This is classic wave behaviour. So what we see is this: in the two-slit experiment the individual electrons arrive like particles in particular

91

places – you can count them in one by one on a detector - but by the time that they have all arrived at the wall they will have distributed themselves in a two-slit wave interference pattern. How can this possibly be?

The double-slit experiment informs us that the electron is apparently behaving as both a wave and a particle (and light particles, photons, behave in the same way). This contradicts what had for centuries been a fundamental tenet of science.

Waves and Particles

It had always been believed that energy could arrive in two forms, either as wave or particle, but never as both simultaneously, since they were exclusive states. A particle goes from A to B, and having left A it must either now have arrived at B, or at some intermediate point between. I cannot say of any particle that it is both at A and at B. This would contradict our perception of reality. But a wave is an oscillating disturbance moving either through space or some other medium. It does not need to transpose matter from A to B; it can move energy from A to B while leaving the original matter at either place. A wave might have begun its motion a hundred miles away across the ocean, but the present disturbance I am witnessing before me is constituted entirely by local water. So the wave can be at A and B at the same time. One sees why the two states were thought to be mutually exclusive.

We know for certain that the electrons arriving for the double-slit experiment are particles. We can even count them if we choose, but we have also seen how they finally form patterns of diffraction and interference. In other words they are making wave patterns. Depending on what measurement we make, we might be observing the electron as a particle or as a wave.

The double-slit experiment appears to be informing us that the electron is behaving both as a wave and as a particle.

2

For centuries scientists had argued about the nature of light – was it a particle (or a corpuscle, as Newton would have said) or was it a wave? Newton thought it was probably a particle, Huygens and Euler a wave. Thomas Young in the early nineteenth century created a very primitive double-slit experiment and established that it was a wave. Later on, waves became more and more important in analysing the rudiments of matter; in Clerk Maxwell's electromagnetic world, waves are at the root of everything. Then, in the early part of the twentieth century, it was discovered, to everyone's astonishment, that light is in fact both wave and particle.

It was in 1900 that Planck postulated that light energy is granular, which is to say that it arrives, not in a continuous stream, but in quanta (small packets) known as photons. These tiny units are what give us the name and identity of quantum physics, and there were many more implications to his discovery than Planck realized at the time. Electromagnetic radiation, for example, could only be received or emitted in certain fixed quantities. What we perceive as a continuous stream of light is in fact discontinuous; it is made up of photons. In which case we now knew for certain that light was made up of particles. So surely that meant it couldn't very well be a wave as well, could it? But the answer to that question is in fact a decided 'Yes'. Nature responds to alternative modes of questioning with different answers. It is reported that on her deathbed, Gertrude Stein was asked by her long-time companion Alice B. Toklas, 'What's the answer, Gertrude?'

To which Gertrude sensibly replied, 'Well, what's the question, Alice?' She was exemplifying complementarity.

3

Let us return to the two-slit experiment with electrons and see how it has profound philosophical implications for us all. We can never predict the individual behaviour of any of the particles; where they will actually end up against that wall. Imagine two physicists, A and B, setting up the experiment identically in different parts of the world, letting electrons through one by one, and recording their arrival points. There would be absolutely no correlation between the arrival point of the first electron in A's experiment and that of the first electron in B's; nor the second, nor the third. However, the final patterns of arrival – see *Fig. 2* above – would be the same for both.

Now here is the key to understanding one crucial aspect of complementarity: we can forecast the overall behaviour of particles in massive numbers (what we might call the **statistical model**), but we can never know where an individual particle will arrive (the **dynamic model**). Or, to put the matter differently, we can foretell the patterns of probability, but never the arrival points of an individual particle. Such unresolvability at the heart of matter has come to alter the way we think of reality. It has put a question mark over the whole issue of causality and determinism. We must look back a little into scientific history to see if we can situate this dilemma in a longer perspective.

Classical Determinism

Let us think about Laplace.

Laplace once boasted that, given the 'initial conditions' – the position and velocity of every particle in the universe at one instant – he could, in principle, predict the future with absolute certainty. This was based on Newton's Second Law of Motion: if at some instant we know (1) the position of an object, and (2) its speed and direction of motion, then, using Newton's Second Law, which tells us how the motion of an object is changed by a force, we can predict its future motion with inevitability and exactitude.

Modern physics has shown this to be untrue. It has demonstrated that at the very heart of matter, and therefore at the centre of any physical system at all, there is a dynamic which is unpredictable. The unfolding of reality can never be foretold in the manner Laplace once imagined it could. Determinism in his sense, based upon a strict, predictable causality, is quite simply impossible, and the reason why this is so is one aspect of complementarity. The mystery that constitutes the essence of modern physics displays itself for us here in the double-slit experiment.

Let us examine two logical terms: causality and contingency. Causality is the kingdom of necessity; what must happen happens. So what is contingency? Contingency is the realm in which it might happen, but doesn't have to. It might not happen, but it could. When an accountant sets up a 'contingency fund', he is allowing for possibilities as yet unforeseen. Now what Laplace was saying about systems and their predictability was that he could translate all contingency into causality, given sufficient information. Some even transposed this unlimited causality to human behaviour, concluding that all of our actions are therefore predetermined. This is classical determinism, and it held sway for a long time; but no longer. Unpredictability in the movements of elementary particles, shown in the double-slit experiment, enshrines contingency at the very heart of reality.

And there is a further caveat. This is in relation to the observer and the observing machinery. Niels Bohr (who first formulated the Principle of Complementarity) said that the apparatus must be seen as part of the phenomenon. What does this mean? Heisenberg's famous Uncertainty Principle (another aspect of complementarity) establishes a simple law in regard to the atomic world: we can observe the velocity of a particle or its position, but not both simultaneously. The reason is that the energy we bring to bear on the observed object changes the state of that object. The energy contained in the light I shine to see where a particle is alters its state (defined by its position and velocity) by injecting new energy into it.

All energy has its effect. If I go out into my garden and shine a torch at the moon, I have directed a certain amount of energy into the cosmos, even though the cosmos contained that energy in the first place. But my torch shone at the moon does not represent enough energy to alter the celestial body I wish to observe; nor would a high energy cosmic ray photon (or gamma ray). But such a gamma ray hitting an electron would knock it clean out of the atom.

A spiralling track such as the one shown in *Fig. 4* (approximately life-size) is a common feature of bubble chamber pictures. They are produced when an electron is knocked out of a hydrogen atom in a tank of liquid hydrogen. As the electron forces its way through the liquid it heats it, making it boil, and leaving a trail of bubbles in its wake. (The curving is produced by a magnetic field.)

In the atomic and subatomic worlds, the seeing alters the seen.

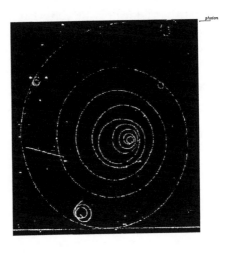

Fig. 4: Spiralling electron tracks in bubble chamber

4

'We are suspended in language,' Bohr often remarked. In trying to express scientific truths we employ language, and language is inherently metaphoric. It is important that we understand this before proceeding, because the problem – it might even be an opportunity – will recur. A crude form of scientific triumphalism once asserted that the language of science presented the literal truth, whereas art in its linguistic form was merely decorative. This was the essence of Thomas Sprat's mission to dispense with what he called 'this vicious abundance of phrase' – he was actually speaking of metaphor - when he wrote his *History of the Royal Society*. During the early part of the twentieth century, there was a movement in philosophy and linguistics which has since been dubbed 'the linguistic turn'. One aspect of this movement acknowledged that all language is inherently metaphorical; that there is no escape from 'metaphorical richness' to 'literal plainness'. Much of Wittgenstein's later philosophy is concerned to make us aware of the extent to which the inherent metaphors in the language we use prompt our thoughts in one direction or another, without our even being aware of the fact. Language itself is here foregrounded, not as the neutral medium through which truth might pass, but as a shaping and structuring world which the speaker, writer and thinker is forced to inhabit. If we are 'suspended in language', then the nature of that language dictates the circumstance of our suspension.

Much of what we call modernism in the arts asserted the supremacy of form. Once again the medium wasn't neutral, existing as a realist device for the unproblematical transmission of a truth content, but was in itself the bearer of form, the very manner of truth's transmission. Artistic form was no longer a matter of surface detail, or the mimicking procedures of illusionism, however exquisitely turned: it determined and structured the truth of the content within it.

This is curious, because at exactly the same time, in a scientific parallel, quantum mechanics was asserting the supremacy of form in reality. The quantum revolution discovered that the world is not one of infinite attenuation, as classical physics had supposed, but is a world of identifiable forms, even if those forms are statistical and probabilistic. An atom can take this form and this energy or that form with that energy, but nothing in-between. In fact there is no 'in-between'; 'in-between' here is an impossibility we play with, so as to try to understand what the real possibilities actually are. If a particle is in the ground state, then a fixed amount of energy is required for it to shift to one of the excited states above it. If the energy provided is less than that, it will not be accepted. There is this form and that one; things are either thus or thus; the nothing that lies between them is not truly expressible even as 'nothing'.

But we remember that our way of looking in the microcosmic world is also structuring the reality as it is perceived. Just as philosophy foregrounded language in the linguistic turn, and the modernist arts foregrounded form, so physics foregrounded its own method of observation in complementarity. The apparatus, said Bohr, must be regarded as part of the phenomenon. The observing/measuring process affects what is being examined.

A thought experiment. Let us make a hydrogen atom, by putting an electron near a proton. Wave-particle complementarity allows us to regard a hydrogen atom as a confined electron wave. We know about confined waves from music: only certain notes (frequencies) can be played on a string, and these are notes with wavelengths that match the length of the string. The string can only be in states that play certain frequencies, while others are not allowed: frequency, in other words, is quantized.

And it is the same in the hydrogen atom: the electron can only exist in certain quantum states which have characteristic shapes and well-defined energies (see *Fig. 5* below); nothing in-between is allowed. There is no in-between. Things are thus or thus.

And here we have another radical peculiarity. The quantum world is full of them. If, in our attempt to find out how these particles passing through our double-slit, one by one, end up as interference patterns, we set up some equipment so that we can monitor which hole each electron actually passes through – for example, we could scatter light from the electrons as they emerge from the slits - the interference patterns disappear. The mystical explanation for this is that the electrons choose not to be observed so closely; the unmystical explanation is that we are once again bringing energy to bear upon the situation and altering it. The apparatus is part of the phenomenon. Scattering light (photons) from the electrons disturbs them enough to smear out the interference pattern.

Now we return to metaphor, and see why it is so important to understand that we are 'suspended in language' and that language is never neutral. When Bohr and Rutherford first created their 'solar system' model of the inside of the atom, they were in effect creating a form of metaphoric perception. This is very common in science. The difference between the use of metaphor in literature and science is largely this: in literature the metaphor often decays into cliché; in science it is usually tested to destruction, then replaced. Let us try to be a little more exact about our use of metaphor here, since it is being asked to cover a large ground.

A metaphor brings together two elements of dissimilarity which nevertheless can be perceived to share elements of similarity. In the dissonance between the dissimilarity and the similarity we generate an intellectual energy which is provocative of thought. 'The moon is a balloon' the singer tells us, and we accept what is in one sense an inherently ludicrous comparison because of a number of striking points of similarity. Both objects are round(ish), and the balloon is trying to rise into the sky. The fact that we know the moon is not 'floating away', but is held in its orbit by the pull of gravity, does not invalidate the momentary perception of the singer, particularly if he is informing us that he is in love and therefore, in an age-old tradition, sees all celestial bodies as shining upon him, and winking at his good fortune, which appears to be ballooning by the minute.

The metaphor is neither the moon nor the balloon; it is the compounding of the two into a single phrase or image. Science uses metaphor in a similar way: it says, let us say that 'this' is 'that', and see what happens. To say that 'this' is 'that' makes us think very closely about what we mean by 'that' and to see to what extent 'this' really corresponds to it. We can only pursue the model, only examine the metaphoric connections and interactions, for as long as they retain some credibility. Science is provisional, in that it always puts itself to the test by checking hypotheses against experiments. If it ceases to do so, it ceases to be science. And this is precisely what happened with the Rutherford-Bohr model. Let us say that 'this' is 'that'. Let us say that the inside of the atom is a miniature version of the solar system. The nucleus was seen as the sun, since it was a massive entity at the heart of the atom. Except for one thing: the more the metaphor was looked into, the more ragged the model it presupposed became. In science the rapid exhaustion of a metaphor means that great progress is being made.

Why did the metaphoric interactions wear out so quickly? Well, if electrons were really orbiting the nucleus as planets orbit the sun, then they would be losing energy constantly in the process – this is what Maxwell's electromagnetism tells us. But if they were constantly losing energy, then the electrons would spiral into the nucleus and the atom would not form. So how is it then that the electrons don't make it down as far as the nucleus? The answer to that question lies in wave-particle complementarity and the quantum states. These images (*Fig. 5*) are not photographs but pictorial representations of the results of quantum mechanical calculations. They show

Fig. 5: Images of the quantum states – the fundamental shapes of nature

the shapes that atomic quantum states can take. The molecules that are made when atoms combine – for example, when two hydrogen atoms and an oxygen atom combine to make a water molecule – must reflect these shapes. Every water molecule is the same because of this – the lines joining the centres of the hydrogen atoms to the centre of the oxygen atom make an angle of about 105 degrees with each other. So these quantum states are the fundamental forms that determine what kind of matter can be produced in nature. That scientists can meaningfully talk about how the Universe has evolved, or can 'create' new materials not yet discovered in nature, is a consequence of the immutable nature of these quantum states. (Not one of these states allows the electron to reside on the nucleus.)

5

Contraria sunt complementa: this was the legend that Bohr incorporated into his own device when he was awarded the Danish Order of the Elephant.

Fig. 6: Niels Bohr's Coat of Arms

Contraria sunt complementa: contraries complement one another. What can this mean? It connects with another statement of Bohr's: that all great truths are equally true the other way around; that the contradiction of any great truth is also valid. This only applies to great truths though, not superficial ones. We must look for a moment at the notion of contradiction.

The word *contradict* comes to us from the Latin *contra* and *dictare:* to say against, to gainsay. In a logical system a contradiction signifies error. If a classical physicist made two statements, that firstly, **P** is a particle, and secondly, **P** is a wave, then assuming we are speaking of the same **P**, both statements cannot be true, since the condition of being a wave excludes the simultaneous possibility of being a particle. In the system of classical physics, **P** could either be described as wave or particle, but not both, not if wave and particle are defined (as they were) as mutually exclusive modes of travel for energy. And yet the double-slit experiment demonstrates over and over that electrons and photons behave as both particles and waves. How could we possibly come to terms with this? *Contraria sunt complementa*. We had to stop thinking either/or, and think instead both/and. It might be worth acknowledging that this has altered the notion of thinking itself. We have entered the new age of quantum enlightenment. Quantum mechanics has generated its own quantum logic. And we might also need to consider what we mean when we name something.

Parenthesis on Naming

For thousands of years we have tried to name the elementals: those rudimentary facts of nature beyond which we cannot go: earth, water, fire and air. They were thought for many centuries to be the ultimate ingredients of matter and energy – the elements. We don't think so now.

Water we say isn't an element; it's a molecular compound. Two atoms of hydrogen combine with one of oxygen and the molecular structure produced is what we call water. Even at the time of Lavoisier, scientists were still thinking of fieriness as a separable substance which permitted the flaming of certain entities. The name for this substance at this time was phlogiston. Now if there was something called phlogiston which burnt away during the fire, then presumably the substance after the burning should be lighter than the substance before. Measure it then: the clarion call of modern science. Take a small measurable aspect of reality; observe and quantify it: this is the key to experimental science since Galileo, and it is what set Galileo so firmly in opposition to Aristotle. In fact it was soon discovered that if you slow-burn tin in a sealed container, the ash at the end of the process weighs more than the tin you began with. Phlogiston evidently can't have departed then – something had been gained, not lost. So out went phlogiston. Fire is not one of the elements; it is rather an emanation from a chemical process involving a number of elements.

How elemental 'fire' is or isn't depends on our view of reality. Each type of naming involves a different conception of the world. And this is true of all naming processes; the names we assign to reality articulate our conception of the world we inhabit. For a long time we used the word atom (employing its Greek etymology) to mean the last indivisible unit of matter: you couldn't go any further than an atom. Atoms were as infinitesimal as the material world could get. In fact the last hundred years have shown that we can get considerably more infinitesimal than that. We now speak of electrons and quarks. In naming the particles we are assigning identities to the aspects of reality we have uncovered. We are saying that certain aspects of reality are characterized by a certain composition, and we can rediscover such identities over and over again. The perceivable structure has expanded.

Imagine that I say, 'I met Picasso once' and you reply, 'Really? Which one?' One of us is in the wrong language game. Because here 'Picasso' refers to a particular unmistakeable character, a diminutive Spanish genius of the visual arts. To name him is to conjure forth that particular identity; only ignorance could produce confusion. But now imagine I said, 'I met a Spanish painter once' and you replied, 'Really? Which one?' Your question is entirely valid, even though 'Spanish painter' is one accurate description of Picasso. Why the difference? Grammatically we could say the distinction lies between the realm of common nouns and that of proper nouns. A common noun provides us with a generic class; a proper noun with an individual. What does individual mean here? It means an object or being capable of the retention of specific identity. Picasso is identifiable by his work; his face; his lovers; his homes; his statements. But if I remain in the realm of generality, then I cannot attribute specific identity. All I know is that someone paints and is also Spanish. Beyond that I can only speculate.

In the atomic world there is no retention of specific identity, which is why we must try to be clear what we mean by 'naming' in this sphere. Since celestial systems were so often used as the basis of metaphoric models for atomic ones, let us return to this theme. We can identify the specific celestial body we call the Moon by various techniques. Photographic images of its surface, with all its craters and mountains, would make it familiar to the eye of a practised astronomer. So we should be able to distinguish this moon from others in the universe. We should be able to distinguish 'Moon' from 'moon'; this is only possible because of the retention of identity.

In the world of the atom this does not apply. There is no retention of identity for atoms or particles. And this means we cannot meaningfully speak of the history of a particle; only of its state, its position or its velocity. (Here we are being precise: in the quantum world, the state of a particle is given by its position or its velocity – the Heisenberg Uncertainty Principle.) It is meaningless to say this specific carbon atom came from Siberia; that one from North Wales. That is to employ the wrong language. In the atomic world there is no Moon; only moons. There are no proper nouns; only common nouns.

It is important to grasp this because the double-slit experiment provides us with a certain type of information which is only meaningful in the light of this non-retention of identity. If we release particles one by one at the slits, sooner or later diffraction and interference patterns will still appear on the screen. How can this be? Are the individual particles interfering with themselves? A pattern of probability is being built up, a pattern that forces us to think in terms of statistical realities, not dynamic ones. We mustn't carry our metaphoric relations from the macrocosm into the world of the microcosm; if we do we will confuse the issue and find the realities being observed even more baffling than they were to begin with. 'We are suspended in language' – Bohr was right, we are, and for that reason we must be aware of the potency of language, particularly in its metaphoric forms.

6

Fig. 7: Wine glass or two faces?

There are a number of images known as 'figure-ground images', one of the most famous being the 'faces and the wine glass' reproduced here. What characterizes the image is this: depending on what portion of the picture you focus as background, and what as foreground, you will see different things. You will see either two faces or a glass. Switch foreground and background and you will now see the alternative. But you can't see both at once. Either the black background is foregrounding the white glass or the white space is now a background to the black faces. This image operates as an emblem of complementarity. We elect planes of reality for observation; the foregrounded plane to some degree makes the background invisible in formal terms. We can see waves or particles; we can determine the velocity of a particle or its position, but not simultaneously.

What we are looking at here is a process of epistemological selection: the notion that we have to elect a form of knowing, and that it will not be all-inclusive in any of its individual modes. The mode of knowing also has its effect upon the identity of the known: the apparatus is a part of the phenomenon. Laplace never anticipated this. He thought truth could be all-comprehending, encyclopaedic and monocular. He thought that observation could be neutral. He believed that metaphors could ultimately be left out of the description, as fanciful. Reality has turned out to be far more baffling; it doesn't yield itself up for universal comprehension quite so easily. Modern physics has discovered mysteries as profound as anything ever imagined in the arts. It has also found itself in agreement with that most anti-scientific of poets, William Blake: 'the eye altering alters all.'

Figure Credits

Fig. 3 is reproduced by kind permission of Ian Kenyon of the University of Birmingham.

Fig. 4, showing a bubble chamber picture of spiralling electron tracks, is reproduced by kind permission of the University of California, Berkeley.

Fig. 5 is reproduced from H. E. White, *Physical Review*, Vol. 37, 1416 (1931).

Fig. 6 is reproduced by kind permission of the Niels Bohr Institute.